Cambridge Elements

Elements in Ancient and Pre-modern Economies
edited by
Kenneth G. Hirth
The Pennsylvania State University
Timothy Earle
Northwestern University
Emily J. Kate
University of Vienna

READING CREATION MYTHS ECONOMICALLY IN ANCIENT MESOPOTAMIA AND ISRAEL

Eric J. Harvey
Stanford University

Shaftesbury Road, Cambridge CB2 8EA, United Kingdom

One Liberty Plaza, 20th Floor, New York, NY 10006, USA

477 Williamstown Road, Port Melbourne, VIC 3207, Australia

314–321, 3rd Floor, Plot 3, Splendor Forum, Jasola District Centre,
New Delhi – 110025, India

103 Penang Road, #05–06/07, Visioncrest Commercial, Singapore 238467

Cambridge University Press is part of Cambridge University Press & Assessment,
a department of the University of Cambridge.

We share the University's mission to contribute to society through the pursuit of
education, learning and research at the highest international levels of excellence.

www.cambridge.org
Information on this title: www.cambridge.org/9781009559881

DOI: 10.1017/9781009559928

© Eric J. Harvey 2025

This publication is in copyright. Subject to statutory exception and to the provisions of relevant collective licensing agreements, no reproduction of any part may take place without the written permission of Cambridge University Press & Assessment.

When citing this work, please include a reference to the DOI 10.1017/9781009559928

First published 2025

A catalogue record for this publication is available from the British Library

ISBN 978-1-009-55988-1 Hardback
ISBN 978-1-009-55991-1 Paperback
ISSN 2754-2955 (online)
ISSN 2754-2947 (print)

Cambridge University Press & Assessment has no responsibility for the persistence or accuracy of URLs for external or third-party internet websites referred to in this publication and does not guarantee that any content on such websites is, or will remain, accurate or appropriate.

For EU product safety concerns, contact us at Calle de José Abascal, 56, 1°, 28003 Madrid, Spain, or email eugpsr@cambridge.org

Reading Creation Myths Economically in Ancient Mesopotamia and Israel

Elements in Ancient and Pre-modern Economies

DOI: 10.1017/9781009559928
First published online: July 2025

Eric J. Harvey
Stanford University

Author for correspondence: Eric J. Harvey, eric@blindscholar.com

Abstract: Creation myths in the ancient Middle East served, among other things, as works of political economy, justifying and naturalizing materially intensive ritual practices and their entanglements with broader economic processes and institutions. These rituals were organized according to a common ideology of divine service, which portrayed the gods as an aristocratic leisure class whose material needs were provided by human beings. Resources for divine service were extracted from the productive sectors of society and channeled inward to the temple and palace institutions, where they served to satiate the gods and support their human servants. This Element examines various forms of the economics of divine service, and how they were supported in a selection of myths – Atraḫasis, Enki and Ninmaḫ, and Enūma Eliš from Mesopotamia and the story of the Garden of Eden from the southern Levant (Israel).

Keywords: Hebrew Bible, Mesopotamian religion, creation myths, political economy, economics of ritual

© Eric J. Harvey 2025

ISBNs: 9781009559881 (HB), 9781009559911 (PB), 9781009559928 (OC)
ISSNs: 2754-2955 (online), 2754-2947 (print)

Contents

1 Introduction 1
2 Creating Labor in Ancient Mesopotamia 10
3 Creating Labor in Ancient Israel 36
4 Conclusions 68

References 70

1 Introduction

"The people they made, imbued with breath, he set to the toil of the gods and they (the gods) were given rest." These lines from the Babylonian poem *Enūma Eliš* (vi 129–30) summarize the myth's conception of the purpose and the duty of humankind. The hard work that was previously the burden of working-class gods – construction, irrigation, agriculture – would henceforth be the responsibility of the newly created human beings. I refer to this as the labor creation motif, which appears in various forms in Mesopotamian texts throughout the second and first millennia BCE. Another example of the motif arose several hundred miles to the West, in the mythology of the Iron Age southern Levant (or, more popularly, ancient Israel).[1] Here, common ingredients borrowed from the Mesopotamian myths were seasoned with local flavor and attributed to the Israelite deity Yahweh: "Yahweh Elohim planted a garden in Eden, in the East … (he) took the human and settled him in the garden to work it and to keep it" (Genesis 2:8,15). Here, too, the human was made to perform the work of cultivation for a god, so that god might rest.

In different forms, then, multiple societies in the ancient Middle East propounded the labor creation motif: that god(s) created human beings for the express purpose of providing labor and service to their creator(s). This idea fit into a broader ideology of divine service, which held that gods were beings with physical needs: food, shelter, clothing, and rest among them. It was the duty of humankind to provide for these needs ritually and materially, and the ideology was enacted daily in public and institutional religious life. Temples were the focus of this service, represented and operated as luxurious houses for the gods, with

---

[1] Though broadly familiar, the designation "ancient Israel" is not without problems. In many ways, it is an illusory construct (or perhaps a constellation of constructs) created by the Hebrew Bible's grand narrative sources and their interpreters. The idea that all of the different tribal groups in the region descend from a legendary common ancestor named Israel (Jacob) and originally shared a common revealed religion must be considered fictional in light of the archaeological evidence. Such claims often say more about the interests of later audiences than actual events in the ancient Levant. As Staples (2021) argues, "by constructing a 'biblical Israel,' the biblical authors, editors, and compilers were able to create a mythic common past and a descriptive lexicon for a present people upon which later communities could build their own identities in continuity with that storied past."

> In this study, I use "ancient Israel" to designate those communities and polities who venerated, worshipped, and performed the service of a deity named Yahweh (exclusively or alongside other deities) in the southern Levant from the beginning of the Iron Age (ca. 1200 BCE) through the destruction of the second Jerusalem temple (70 CE), especially when discussing portrayals in the biblical text. In contrast, I tend to use "the southern Levant" when discussing archaeological discoveries, whose association with any parties or peoples mentioned in the Hebrew Bible cannot be presumed. The distinction, I hope, makes clear that the Hebrew Bible emerged from the southern Levantine context but does not represent it fully or accurately.

personnel and activities focused on the care and feeding of their divine residents. This involved, among other things, the construction and ornamentation of the temple buildings themselves, the care of the gods' statues, clothing, and accessories, and the preparation and service of daily and festival meals. As such, divine service had substantial material requirements and economic ramifications that encompassed all of society. As Tzvi Abusch writes: "The purpose of human life, the purpose of the community, was to serve the gods, to provide them with whatever care a powerful ruling class, a landed aristocracy, would require. Paramount among these needs are shelter and food" (Abusch, 2020: 57).

In this Element, I examine how the economics of ritual operated and were justified by ideology and myth in Mesopotamia from the Old Babylonian period through the Seleucid Era (ca. seventeenth–second c. BCE) and in the southern Levant from the Iron Age to the Hellenistic period (ca. twelfth–fourth c. BCE). Divine service functioned as a focal point and structuring force for economic activity in all of these contexts, mobilizing substantial resources to supply rituals and support the personnel who performed them. I devote particular attention to the special role of creation mythology in naturalizing and upholding the divine service economy. To this end, I explore the economic perspective and ramifications of four related myths: the *Atraḥasis Epic*, *Enki and Ninmaḥ*, and *Enūma Eliš* from Mesopotamia, and the Garden of Eden story (also known as the Yahwistic primeval history) from the southern Levant. Each region and time period exhibits its own unique character, but several key features of ritual, economy, ideology, and mythology were shared across the ancient Middle Eastern world. I begin, therefore, with some introductory comments on temple rituals, ancient Middle Eastern economics, and creation mythology in comparative perspective.

1.1 Temples, Palaces, and the Ideology of Divine Service

The concept of divine service in the ancient Middle East differed from the use of the term "service" in religious contexts today, where the term usually denotes a formal ceremony for communal worship. It is much closer to the term as it is used in Victorian and Edwardian dramas: as the duties of lower strata in the household hierarchies of the landed aristocracy. Service refers to the work of servants – all of the duties performed on a practical level to see to the maintenance of a manor house and the feeding, clothing, bathing, and provisioning of the house's upper-class occupants.

This is especially appropriate considering the representation of temples as houses for the gods, organized along the lines of extended aristocratic estates (Selz, 2007; Boer, 2015). Indeed, most of the terminology for temples in the languages of the ancient Middle East overlaps with that used for human habitations – houses, palaces, dwellings, and even tents. Within this framework, the regular activities of the gods' households take on a different character: reverence and worship, certainly, but combined with the practical work of caretaking.

This understanding reframes many rituals and activities of the temple. The term sacrifice, for example, can be misleading, enmeshed as it has become with concepts like atonement and a fixation on the ritual and spiritual power of death. Christian theology and ritual anthropology, despite their major differences, have both associated sacrifice closely with sacred killing, identifying slaughter itself as the ritual focal point and source of efficacy (McClymond, 2008; Kitts, 2022). In the words of Hubert and Mauss (1964: 35), "through this act of destruction the essential action of sacrifice was accomplished."

Yet many scholars have observed that the most common "sacrifices" described and prescribed in ancient Mesopotamian texts do not fit this framework in the slightest (Lambert, 1993; Bottéro, 2001; Scurlock, 2002, 2006a, 2006b; Pongratz-Leisten, 2012; Stackert, 2012; Brisch, 2017; Abusch, 2020). The most frequent rituals performed in Mesopotamian temples and shrines did not center on the act of killing or derive their primary effect from it, even though they required the slaughter of sometimes extraordinary numbers of animals. Slaughter itself was little more than a prerequisite for the main event, when the animals were butchered, cooked, and served to the gods for their daily meals alongside breads, cakes, fruits, and beer and wine in abundance. This was provisioning, less sacred killing than sacred cooking, and the moment of slaughter was no more the focal point than it is for a fancy banquet or backyard barbecue. Increasingly, the same realization is reaching Levantine and biblical studies, as a substantial subset of sacrificial rituals in the Hebrew Bible are also presented, literally or metaphorically, as meals for the deity (Scurlock, 2006a, 2006b; Feldman, 2020a, 2020b; Hemmer-Gudme, 2020).

For this reason, I refer to these rituals as offerings or, more directly, as provisions or the temple meal service, reserving the term "sacrifice" for rituals in which the act of killing is more central, such as those intended to seal a treaty, atone for sin or guilt, purge impurity, or seek a message from the gods (Scurlock, 2002: 396–403; Pongratz-Leisten, 2012: 292–94).

Like household service, temple service was a profoundly practical endeavor, rooted deeply in material needs and organized through stratified power relationships. Temples were staffed by various kinds of priests and other specialized personnel whose job it was to see to the gods' needs and comfort. These personnel prepared and served the gods' meals, but they also needed to eat. Thus, the gods' meals served a dual function: once presented and consumed ritually by the deity, the food was eaten by the priests and other personnel associated with the temple or shrine, as well as the members of their own households. The manner in which offerings were prepared, divided, and presented differed between Mesopotamia and the Levant, but in both contexts, offerings served both to satiate their divine recipients and to support the human personnel who prepared them.

And just as wealthy landowners and their households were supported by the productive labor of subordinated agricultural workers on and beyond their estate, so temples operated on food and drink produced by laborers within and outside their walls. Ritual professionals did not produce the food they required to live, and neither did the agricultural workers and pastoralists receive equivalent material goods in exchange for their contributions. This is where questions of ideology and political economy come in, as the temple's acquisitive demands needed to be justified, naturalized, and reinforced.

1.2 Divine Service and the Broader Economy

The call of divine service radiated outward from the temple, demanding participation from all of society. As such, it functioned as an organizing principle for a broad array of economic practices and processes. This should not be overstated, as a great deal of economic activity always occurred outside of the divine service economy, but it nevertheless played a powerful role across time and space. I begin, therefore, with a general theoretical orientation and some common features of ancient economies.

I approach the economy as an expansive and holistic phenomenon, largely consonant with Karl Polanyi's definition of the substantive meaning of economics, which "derives from man's dependence for his living upon nature and his fellows. It refers to the interchange with his natural and social environment, in so far as this results in supplying him with the means of material want satisfaction" (Polanyi, 1957: *xx*). In other words, the economy is not something that can be unmoored from broader social, political, or religious structures and approached as a discrete and isolated locus of inquiry (Polanyi, 1944, 1957; Boer, 2015). Every act of the production, mobilization, and transfer of labor and material goods is embedded within social systems, institutions, and relationships. This basic tenet of substantivist economics has stood the test of time, though Polanyi has been rightly critiqued on specifics. His reduction of economic processes to three basic categories (reciprocity, redistribution, and exchange), for example, is overly simplistic and must be supplemented by considerations of production, hierarchy, extraction, and class. This general approach to the study of economics, then, benefits from the critiques and theoretical refinements provided by economic anthropologists (Earle, 2002;

Hirth, 2023) and Marxist scholars (Boer, 2015, 2023). Each of these brings important concepts and analytical tools to bear on the problems of ancient economies, and I employ aspects of their analysis without dogmatic reliance on one over the others.

All of these researchers tend to divide between the most basic work of subsistence in ancient economies and the more complex forms that developed to address the use of surplus. Earle (2002) draws a basic distinction between the subsistence economy and the political economy. Hirth (2023) distinguishes between the domestic economy and an institutional economy with informal and formal sectors. Boer (2015, 2023) describes survival-subsistence activity as one of two allocatory institutional forms (along with kinship household), which differ fundamentally from the extractive institutional forms of estate and tribute exchange.

Subsistence was the backbone of all ancient economies, as it is today, but in ancient societies a far greater proportion of the population was always engaged in producing the basic necessities of food and fiber (Hirth, 2023). This work was done in domestic contexts or small kinship groups, where labor and resources were allocated according to need, ability, and social convention (Boer, 2015: 46–7, 49–51; Hirth, 2023: 20–1). Unlike modern market economies, where almost everyone relies for survival on trade in goods they are unable to produce, small kinship-based communities could grow or make most of what they needed to survive among themselves. For this reason, many families successfully maintained their livelihoods through survival-subsistence strategy as an institutional form (Sasson, 2010: 7–48; Boer, 2023: 44–7). This formed a durable economic base layer that supported more complex economic forms and persisted even when regimes collapsed.

Depending on the environmental and technological factors at play, communities were often able to produce some level of surplus. The concept of surplus, heuristically understood as the amount of production in excess of a community's survival needs, has recently come under renewed scrutiny (Morehart and De Lucia, 2015). Though excess production is important, framing questions in this way obscures the choices that precede production or engender changes in production strategy.

Consequently, I find it more generative to frame surplus in terms of excess time and energy – that is, as a reduction in the total labor share of a community required to meet their barest subsistence needs. A community of a certain size has a finite amount of time and energy to commit to labor, and as the ability to produce grows, the amount of that labor needed to feed, clothe, and shelter everyone shrinks in proportion to the whole. In this view, the flexibility of surplus takes center stage. Surplus engenders choices and its application is contingent on cultural and historical factors. Stated differently, surplus permits the development of more complex economic forms and institutions atop the survival subsistence layer, but it does not command their character. To say that a certain economic form or institution requires a certain amount of surplus is not the same thing as saying that the surplus necessitates the development of that form.

Thus, complex forms that emerge may be more or less egalitarian or hierarchical. In relatively autonomous households or extended kinship groups, surplus may be turned toward the common good. For example, they may choose to maintain steady production levels and simply work less. Alternatively, they can opt to consume surplus production in communal feasts or to store it as insurance against future misfortune.

Surplus also enables the formation of hierarchical and stratified institutions. In the ancient Middle East specifically, the two most important of these were the temple and the palace. For thousands of years, these two institutions dominated the political economy, adapting and employing various strategies to control and integrate economic activity with more or less success. As Boer notes, both institutions are variations on the basic form of an estate (Boer, 2015: 110–38). The patrimonial household or estate was one of the basic organizational units of society, especially on a symbolic level (Schloen, 2001; Hirth, 2023: 28), and its logic was easily extended to complex social forms and formal institutions. As such, the temple and the palace both represented and organized themselves as extended patrimonial estates, with the head of a palace being its king and the head of a temple its resident god or gods (Sallaberger, 2007; Selz, 2007: 280–1).[2] Considering the divine status of their heads, temples claimed a position of ideological primacy – although in practice they were not always the more powerful of the two.

These institutions formalized the specialization of labor and with it divisions according to class. By this, I refer to groups within a society whose material interests are divergent and antagonistic to one another. The economic component of class is almost always accompanied by other social distinctions, as class influences the nature and scope of interpersonal connections and becomes entangled with any number of other sociological and social-psychological factors (Bourdieu, 1984). Not everyone inside the temple or palace belonged

---

[2] Temples were often dedicated primarily to one god or a divine couple and included shrines or apartments for other deities who were served there in a lesser capacity. In the third millennium Sumerian temples, the specifically gendered aspect of patrimonialism was far more muted than it later became. The primary deity of a temple was often female, and in almost all cases the highest priest of a temple was the opposite gender of the main deity (or, in the case of Inanna's temple, defied gender expectations altogether). For more on gender in Sumerian temples, see Westenholz (2013).

to the upper class or shared in its benefits, but as institutions they were helmed by wealthy elites and served their class interests.

The temple and palace engaged in complex and varied economic activity, but on balance their disposition can rightly be understood as extractive (Boer, 2015, 2023). That is, even when they engaged in reciprocal or redistributive processes, they did so in ways that disproportionately benefited themselves. To the temple and palace, the productive sectors of society were sites from which revenue could be acquired in the form of donations, tithes, conscription, taxes, tribute, and plunder. Their strategies of acquisition spanned a spectrum from voluntary support to coercion and seizure by force (Hirth, 2023: 26–7). To agricultural and pastoral workers, the palace and temple could bring some benefits but with an acquisitiveness that constantly threatened to get out of control (Boer, 2023: 60–1). Formal institutions allowed for increased specialization of labor, greater diversity and quality of goods, and monumental public works, but their costs and benefits were not equally distributed. Menial laborers employed directly by the temple and corvee laborers set to work on royal construction projects were supplied with allocations of grain, oil, and wool, for example, but this remuneration scarcely offset the value of their labor.

The extraction and accumulation of surplus created and intensified economic inequality and with it disparities in economic, social, and political power (Hirth, 2023: 25). As such, these economic arrangements were not self-evidently beneficial to the working classes, and Boer notes how the peasantry may have fared better in times of state crisis and collapse than political stability, since the entities that collapsed were those that expropriated their surplus (Boer, 2023: 61–2). Resistance was a real and constant threat, and the institutions pursued various means to assert and maintain their authority, through force when necessary and through ideologies of (real or imagined) benefit to society. Violence was the backstop of extraction, but the institutional economies ran more smoothly when participation was voluntary. As such, the temple and palace made great efforts to propagate the ideology of divine service. In its fullest articulation, this ideology did not simply concern the houses of the gods, but constructed a model of cosmic society wherein all human activity was oriented toward the maintenance of the gods' comfort. In effect, it situated the gods as the highest socioeconomic class above even the wealthy leaders of the great institutions. Within this model, kings and high priests were removed from the top tier of the societal class structure to mere intermediaries – a kind of professional managerial class serving the true (divine) aristocracy. In this model of the cosmos, the palace and temple funneled resources inward and channeled them upward to the gods, while on the material level, of course, the institutions themselves remained the primary beneficiaries.

1.3 Creation Myths and the Ideology of Divine Service

The ideology of divine service permeated the societies of ancient Mesopotamia and the southern Levant, represented frequently in text, art, and architecture. It is impossible to dwell here on the origins, development, and full expression of this ideology in relation to the great institutions, except to say that one in no way created the other directly. Rather, the two developed together in an ongoing process of social formation, wherein social and economic forms influenced conceptions of the divine and cosmic society and were in turn influenced by them. Social formation as a concept has been productively explored as both product and process in the development of religious and economic forms (Godelier, 1986; McCutcheon, 2024). By the time the labor creation motif begins to appear in the textual record, both the great institutions and the ideology of divine service were well-developed and firmly embedded in societies across the Middle East.

Thus, the labor creation motif and its mythological vessels must be understood as expressions produced by, within, and for a divine service economy. They are particular manifestations of a broader process that scholars of religion call mythmaking. As Russell McCutcheon puts it, "mythmaking is one strategy whereby social formations abstract their beginnings from history, thereby privileging one particular view of the present by linking it to a mythic originary moment" (McCutcheon, 2024: 88). Clearly, this is the crucial contribution of creation mythology: presenting the economic and social landscape familiar to their audiences not as a historically contingent and potentially transitory state of affairs, but as a cosmic order imposed by the gods from the beginning. In this light, the four myths treated herein present a direct line from the realities of temple and palace extraction to the divinely devised design of the cosmic order. In one way or another, each narrates the god(s) creating humankind for the express purpose of providing for their material and social needs. The motif was developed in the most depth and detail by the two oldest exemplars – *Atraḫasis* and *Enki and Ninmaḫ* – both attested from the seventeenth c. BCE (Old Babylonian period) onward. It was then picked up and carried on in a less-prominent position by the later Babylonian composition *Enūma Eliš*. From the southern Levant, only one example of the labor creation motif survives, embedded in the texts of the Hebrew Bible. This is the Garden of Eden narrative (Genesis 2:4b–3:24, which was originally independent of the preceding (and quite different) creation account (Genesis 1:1–2:4a).

As the previous sentence implies, these four myths represent only a small part of the creation mythology from the ancient Middle East. Neither Mesopotamia nor the southern Levant held to a single, fixed, and stable account of the world's origins, and their mythological texts recount creation with a variety of different themes and interests.³ The labor creation motif was, therefore, not universal. It is only one type of mythmaking attested from antiquity, but a type with a particularly clear connection with the material and political economy. Furthermore, these myths did not invent the motif independently. There is also an intertextual aspect, as the younger texts doubtless knew the older ones in some form and adopted the trope for their own purposes. This is perhaps less surprising in relation to the texts that share in the cuneiform literary tradition, but it extends to the biblical materials as well. The scribes of Mesopotamia and the southern Levant participated in an international literary culture characterized by the adaptation and reformulation of common figures, themes, and narrative, and the influence of Mesopotamian literature on the book of Genesis has long been recognized (Tsumura, 1994; Mandell, 2022).

In light of all this, it can be difficult to draw more precise conclusions about the myths' intended purpose, reception, or impact in their ancient contexts. These myths are exercises in mythmaking whose particular expression is informed by interaction with theological systems, sociopolitical and economic forms and institutions, and a history of literary interaction and borrowing. The texts themselves make claims about the origins and purpose of the divine service economy, but it cannot be known from our vantage point how these claims translated into effects on the world. For one thing, it is unclear what type of people represent the intended audience(s) of each myth. As written texts, the surviving versions derived rather tautologically from the most literate strata of society, and much of the populace would have been unable to read them. Apart from *Enūma Eliš*, which was recited in full at various festivals in the late-first millennium BCE (Linssen, 2004: 81, 118), we do not know if these texts or their message were intentionally disseminated. Furthermore, it is hazardous to posit a straightforward connection between the text's claims and the beliefs of ancient peoples. It is simply not possible to know how many residents of Mesopotamia or the Levant believed a given account of creation, and for the purposes of economic organization belief itself is not particularly important. Whether someone plays their prescribed part in an economic institution out of deep devotion, social convention, or simply to avoid punishment, the part is still played and the system trundles on. In the sections that follow, therefore, it will suffice to explore the organization of the divine service economy and to demonstrate that the mythological texts provided an explicit rationalization for its value and necessity.

---

³ For other Mesopotamian myths, see the various texts included in Part Three of Lambert (2013). For the diversity of biblical creation mythology, see the accounts in Genesis 1:1–2:4a and Proverbs 8, along with briefer references in Isaiah 51:9–11 and Psalm 74:2–18 and 136.

10 Ancient and Pre-modern Economies

2 Creating Labor in Ancient Mesopotamia

We begin our journey through temples and texts on the alluvial plain formed by the Tigris and Euphrates rivers, the area known as Mesopotamia (Figure 1).

2.1 Mesopotamian Economies: A View from the Temple

Ancient Mesopotamia provides particularly fertile ground for economic investigation, as most institutional records were kept on clay tablets, hundreds of thousands of which have survived to the present day. These records offer contemporaneous economic and administrative information in a volume and detail unparalleled in the ancient world, covering day-to-day details of labor, resource usage, and other necessary activities. Such records are not comprehensive, as they tend to be associated with temples and palaces – the great institutions of Mesopotamian society – and a great deal of economic activity took place outside of their circle of control and oversight. However, this study examines those very institutions and their mythological self-justifications, so their overrepresentation is less of a concern than it would be in a more holistic economic discussion.

Even with such vast contemporary textual data, many aspects of institutional operations remain elusive. Temple activities were not all described or recorded equally, and the nature of archaeological finds is both chance and partial. At times, information from hundreds of years and miles apart must be combined to reconstruct an entire economic institution or process. Nevertheless, these disparate sources suggest that many structural elements of institutional organization and operation persisted across much of the period of the cuneiform tradition (Bottéro, 2001: 120). Thus, the basic account of the temple and its entanglements with the broader economy that I present here holds true, with some variation, from the mid-third millennium BCE to the end of the first millennium BCE, if not longer. These include: (1) the representation and organization of temples along the lines of aristocratic estates, (2) the central purpose of which was to provide for the material support and comfort of their divine lords with lavish accoutrements, entertainments, and meals, (3) the distribution of the gods' leftovers and other requisitioned goods to feed and support the priests and other temple personnel, and (4) the support of these institutions through a variety of voluntary, compulsory, and coercive strategies of production, extraction, and exchange.

2.1.1 Temples as Houses and Households

By the second millennium BCE, when myths with the labor creation motif began to be attested, palace and temple were both mature and complex institutions deeply engrained within the fabric of settled society. Structures identifiable as

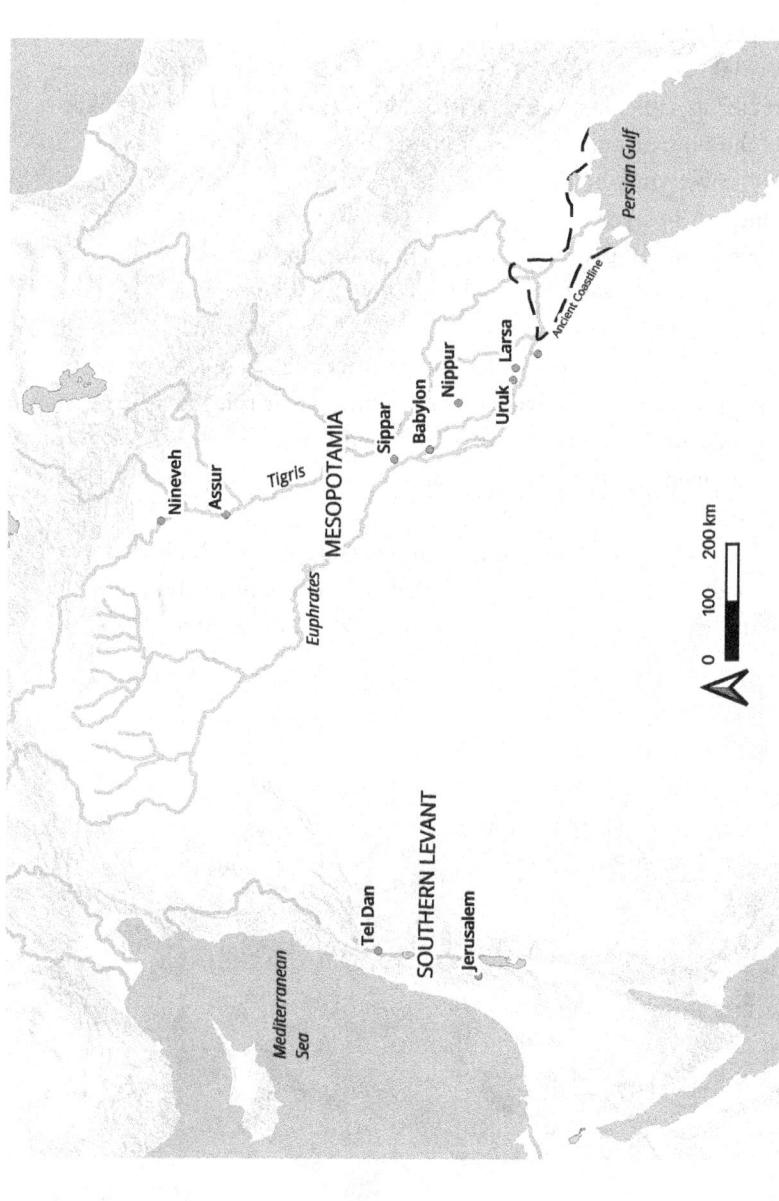

Figure 1 The ancient Middle East. Map by Jessie DeGrado and Eric Harvey. Basemap by ESRI. Approximate location of the gulf in the second and first millennia BCE reconstructed using data from Milli and Forti (2019).

temples appear first in the archaeological record, beginning in the fourth millennium in southern Mesopotamia (Stone, 2013: 157–8). These preceded – and probably catalyzed – the development of large-scale urbanism. Indeed, it is probable that temples originated as (or as part of) sites used for the communal storage of grain for consumption and seed, with surplus banked against future misfortunes (Makkay, 1983; Pollock, 1999: 5, 87–93). Larger storage complexes were constructed as settlements grew, but temples remained administrative hubs that directed the flow of grain and other goods into and out of them. As such, temples were never sites of purely spiritual veneration – from their earliest appearance they also played a central role in the material economy.

Palaces appear later. Early towns and cities seem to have had a single ruler, a priest-king who served what we would call both religious and secular functions. In the third millennium, these two roles diverged, and so did their headquarters. Residences for city rulers begin to enlarge and separate as the institutions defined themselves against one another. Their roles and functions differed and they often competed for power and influence, but these great institutions remained inextricably bound in mutual dependence for resources and legitimation.

Compared to the surrounding domestic architecture, temple buildings were monumental and lavish structures, though they varied widely according to the size and wealth of their town or city (Bottéro, 2001: 114–9; Figure 2). They

Figure 2 Proposed digital reconstruction of the Eanna district in Uruk during the New Year's Festival, as it would have appeared in the Ur III period (21st c. BCE). © 2012, artefacts-berlin.de; Material: German Archaeological Institute.

were also richly appointed with decorations of the highest quality and rarest materials. The resident gods themselves were represented by statues constructed of wood overlaid with precious metals, clothed in luxurious cloth, and ornamented with expensive jewelry (Postgate, 1992: 109–19; Maggio, 2012). They were staffed by a host of officials and servants whose work revolved around the care, feeding, and entertainment of their divine masters. The scope and complexity of temple functions comes across clearly in the standard list of temple professions, which was finalized in the Early Dynastic period and copied for centuries thereafter (Westenholz, 2013: 247). It included more than 250 distinct titles for temple functionaries, ranging from the highest priests and ritual officiants to quotidian personnel such as bakers, weavers, watchmen, and sweepers of the courtyard. No temple employed someone in every office on the list, but the list gives a clear indication of the variety of roles necessary to maintain a temple's daily operations.

2.1.2 The Temple Food service: Menu and Scale

One such regular activity was the provision of food to the deities in the form of their daily meals (Oppenheim, 1977: 183–97; Postgate, 1992: 119–122; Lambert, 1993: 194; Bottéro, 2001: 125–32; Scurlock, 2002, 2006a, 2006b; Linssen, 2004: 129–66; Pongratz-Leisten, 2012; Stackert, 2012; Abusch, 2020). Gods expected to be fed several times per day. The number of meals and their size and content varied according to local custom but always included at least one morning and one evening meal. Though some special terminology does exist for the gods' provisions, they are just as often described in the same words as human meals (Lambert, 1993: 196–7).

Mealtimes could be elaborate events (Figure 3). Officiating priests placed the food on stands set before the statues of the gods in choreographed sequence, accompanied by ritualized recitations, music, and other entertainments.[4] The substance of the actual meal was dictated pragmatically according to local foodways and the size and wealth of the temple's city. In general, the menu would have resembled the fine foods enjoyed by human elites: meat from cattle, sheep, goats, fish, birds, and game along with grains, vegetables, fruits, and large quantities of beer, wine, and dairy.[5]

---

[4] For one example, see the text KAR 154 (Menzel, 1981, vol. 2, T 2ff.; Pongratz-Leisten, 2012: 296), in which directions for the presentation of food are intermixed with ritual instructions for the *qadištu*-women who recite *inḫu*-songs before the divine statues and the *šangû*-priest who performs various purifications. The text also contains instructions for the disposal or distribution of leftovers at the end.

[5] The exceptions to this rule involve goat and pork, which were served to gods much less often than they were consumed by people (Lambert, 1993: 198; Scurlock, 2002, 2006a: 35). Pigs were

Figure 3 A Neo-Assyrian (ninth to eighth century BCE) cylinder seal depicting a cultic banquet scene. Photo © 2024, The Metropolitan Museum of Art.

Enough prescriptive and descriptive texts concerning these ritual meals are attested from various times and places to prove their antiquity,[6] but some of the most detailed and complete examples come from late in the cuneiform tradition. One such group of texts details the proper service of Anu and the other gods in the Eanna temple at Uruk (Thureau-Dangin, 1921: 74–86; Linssen, 2004: 172–83). One especially informative tablet (TU 38) was produced in the Seleucid Era (ca. 261 BCE), though it claims to have copied an early Neo-Babylonian original.[7] According to this document, all of the gods of the temple received four daily

---

offered only in rites associated with the netherworld or its deities, perhaps because they were thought of as dirty and defiling creatures. Goats may simply have been considered too common for divinities. Sometimes, a certain temple would also avoid serving certain gods specific foods. The Late Babylonian text discussed below prohibited serving mutton to Šakkan, beef to Ningublaga, fowl to Bēlet-ṣēri, and both beef and fowl to Ereškigal in the Eanna temple at Uruk (Thureau-Dangin, 1921: 74–86). Menus sometimes omit fresh fruits and vegetables, more likely because they varied seasonally than because they were absent from the meals (Lambert, 1993: 198).

[6] Examples from earlier periods include: for Old Babylonian, Dossin (1938) and Kingsbury (1963); Middle Assyrian, Menzel (1981), Pongratz-Leisten (2012).

[7] The text is TU 38 = *Racc.* 62 8 and 74 8, published in Thureau-Dangin (1921), translated into English by Sachs (1969: 343–5), and treated subsequently by Linssen (2004: 172–83) and Waerzeggers (2010). In the tablet's colophon, the scribe claims to have copied this tablet from ones he encountered in Elam, where they had been taken by Nabopolassar (reigned 626–605 BCE). The historical problems with this colophon are several, and it is likely an attempt by the Seleucid Era Anu priesthood to emphasize the importance of their cult by anchoring it in an already ancient tradition (Da Riva, 2017: 78–9). As Robbins (1996: 78) notes, these prescriptive texts also do not align easily with tabular records of provisions from Uruk in the decades spanning the end of Neo-Babylonian and the beginning of Achaemenid Persian rule.

meals – one large and one small meal in the morning and the same in the evening. The obverse of the tablet specifies the required amounts of beverage (beers, milk, and wine), breads, and dried fruits, and the reverse is devoted to meat and changes for special calendrical occasions. Rather than reproducing the entire 100-line menu here, I present only a taste: the daily drinks for Anu alone and the daily meat total for all the gods (translation adapted from Linssen, 2004: 172–83).

> Every day of the entire year, for the main meal of the morning, you will arrange, in addition to the *šappu*-containers of the libation bowls, eighteen golden *šappu*-containers on the offering table of Anu. Of these (eighteen containers) you will arrange in the presence of Anu: seven *šappu*-containers on the right, three with barley-beer, four with *labku*-beer, (and) seven *šappu*-containers on the left, three with barley-beer, one with *labku*-beer, one with *nāšu*-beer, one with *zarbābu*-beer, and milk in an alabaster *šappu*-container, (and) four golden *šappu*-containers with drawn wine.
> For the second meal of the morning and the main and second meal of the evening: ditto, but no milk will be served for the main and second meal of the evening. (obv. 1–7)
>
> ...
>
> Totaling, every day of the whole year, for the four meals of the day: twenty-one fat, pure, first-quality sheep that have been fed barley for two years; four *kalû*-sheep for the regular offering, (fattened) with milk; Twenty-five 'lower' sheep of lesser quality which have not been fed barley; two full-grown oxen; one suckling calf; eight lambs; thirty *marratu*-birds; thirty turtledoves; three geese that have been fed dough; five ducks that have been fed dough(!); two ducks of lesser quality; four *ušummu*-mice; three ostrich eggs; three duck eggs. (rev. 24–9)

The meat and drink were supplemented by grain and fruits: 168 loaves of bread from around 650 liters of barley flour and another 1,200 oil-fried cakes topped with around 650 liters of dates. On festival days, celebrated monthly, annually, and on significant occasions, these regular meals were bolstered further by special offerings (Robbins, 1996: 69–78; Linssen, 2004: 40–127; and see Scurlock, 2002: 391, for other times and temples).

The sheer quantity of food indicated in this text is breathtaking. And while it is true that the numbers in these prescriptive texts do not always match the totals in accounting and bookkeeping records (Robbins, 1996: 79), the Eanna seems to have routinely served approximately 4,300 sheep to the gods per year (Kozuh, 2014: 1).[8] Eanna was a major temple in a large city, and others may not have matched its scale. The volume of daily meals would have varied widely from

---

[8] Though they are not as explicit in regard to the culinary nature of offerings, economic and administrative records of the receipt, transfer, and disbursal of animals, grain, and other foodstuffs

place to place and time to time. Nevertheless, the food given to the gods in Mesopotamian temples was usually sufficient to feed a large number of people – which is exactly what it did.

2.1.3 The Gods' Leftovers, the Servants' Food

The gods' table was not the last stop for these dishes. Once the meals had been ritually prepared, served, and (symbolically) consumed by the deities, the "leftovers" were cleared away and distributed for consumption by temple officials and personnel (Linssen, 2004: 139; Brisch, 2017; Abusch, 2020: 59). The gods' portions themselves went to the highest priests and, in many cases, to the king and his family in the palace (Beaulieu, 1990). Texts provide detailed information regarding who received which cut of meat and which portion of other dishes. Sometimes these instructions are appended to ritual instructions themselves and other times the information was relayed on its own. Take, for example, this brief extract from a longer Neo-Assyrian list of meat disbursals (Kataja and Whiting, 1995: 81, lines 4–17):

> [I]he inner cuts, left thigh, blade-bone, two joints of the backbone, four ribs: all for the House of Many Kings.
> A haunch: the mausoleum of Ešarra-ḥamat
> The right thigh: the high priest.
> Four ribs: the second priest
> Four ... coverings of thighs, four joints of the backbone: the priest of Ea-šarri.
> The neck: the lamentation chanter.
> A shoulder: the temple scribe.

The reverse contains different distributions to many of the same parties, suggesting their diets varied from day to day.

Temple food did not only go to gods, kings, and priests, however. As Brisch (2017: 51) writes: "Temples were responsible for feeding the gods, but also for sustaining a substantial part of the city community." Lower-rank temple personnel and dependents also received food income from the temple kitchens. Scholars refer to these distributions as "prebends," job-specific entitlements to certain cuts of meat and specified amounts of bread, beer, and other staples (Waerzeggers, 2010: 77–102). It was these workers who justified the amounts of food dedicated to the gods' meals.

However, prebends were also hereditary and could be divided between inheritors. Over time, a large prebend could be divided into smaller and

---

provide much more comprehensive information about their economic impact. For some examples, see Kozuh (2014), Kataja and Whiting (1995: 80–1), Sigrist (1984), Robbins (1996), and Brisch (2017).

smaller parts that became insufficient to support one person, let alone a family. Those at the top of the temple hierarchy lived in luxury, but for those at the bottom possessing a prebend was no guarantee of wealth or comfort. As with many large, extractive organizations, the fact that they siphoned surplus from outside their walls did not mean they avoided exploiting those within.

The consumption of divine leftovers ties the symbolic and material functions of the temple together in a way that clarifies the institution's rhetorical usefulness. On the symbolic plane, the gods were the heads of household, and the priests and kings were simply the top tier of their service staff – a kind of transmundane Professional Managerial Class. Materially, it was these priests and kings who benefitted first and foremost from the temple's collection of resources from the broader society. In other words, those at the top of the social hierarchy placed themselves in the middle of a cosmic class structure in ways that justified their acquisitive tendencies and relieved them of responsibility for any of the system's shortcomings. This proved very useful in the integration of the temple regime into the broader economy.

2.1.4 Supporting the Estate

The smooth functioning of Mesopotamian temples required that food and other resources of the right kind and sufficient quantity be available when they were needed. Like households of the human gentry, the gods' houses were not supported through the activities of the household servants alone, but through their more extended holdings – the difference of course being that the gods' estates encompassed all of human society. On a social and political level, the institutions of Mesopotamian society worked together to siphon surplus from the productive sectors of the economy using a variety of extractive means, from the voluntary to the coercive and the ambiguous in-between.

Temple extraction emerged from the very early (prehistoric) collocation of sacred sites with communal seed and surplus storage (Makkay, 1983). From there, the temple's economic activities grew and diversified, incorporating a wide variety of revenue streams. These varied, of course, by time period, and I can only offer some representative generalities here.

In every period, temples welcomed voluntary gifts (Sumerian arua, Akkadian širku) from private citizens (Mieroop, 1989: 398–9; Kataja and Whiting, 1995: 92–8). Some festivals seem to have occasioned such gifts (Lambert, 1993: 194–5), which could be scaled according to the offeror's means (Oppenheim, 1956: 340). Thus, gifts could range from a bird or basket of grain to entire estates with attached fields, houses, and resident laborers (Kataja and Whiting, 1995: 98).

Individuals given to a temple as arua or *širku* became bound laborers who were not free to leave the temple but could also not be bought or sold like chattel.

Many gifts came directly from the king. These included regular provisions for the daily food service as well as precious trade goods, valuable votive objects, and new or renewed temple construction (Lambert, 1993: 195). In the Neo-Babylonian period, for example, Nebuchadnezzar II described his increased food provisions to the head divine couple of Babylon, Marduk, and Zarpanitu, providing them with one fattened bull, five sheep, three fish, assorted birds and rodents, eggs, ghee, oil, honey, and wine "as plentiful as river water" (Langdon, 1912: 90–4). One-time gifts and bequests were commemorated as signs of exceptional piety or acts anticipating divine favor in return (Kataja and Whiting, 1995: 86–91).

Temples that accrued significant wealth could then leverage it to their own advantage. They purchased slaves with rare skills, such as dyeing and weaving multi-colored cloth (Kataja and Whiting, 1995: 94), and made loans that could be repaid in silver or in food/drink resources (Brisch, 2017: 48). Interest on these loans could provide profit for the institution, but they were also sometimes offered at zero percent interest as a form of public charity.

Such voluntary measures did not yield as much support as mandatory contributions backed by the threat of force, however. The freewill gifts of the king especially mask coercive and violent practices. Some precious goods were acquired by trade, but others (as well as staples) were collected through taxation or seized as plunder. At the end of the third millennium, the Ur-III state administered a system of rotational taxation known as bala, in which the provinces each took turns contributing to a central coffer for part of each year. This fund was used for several purposes: to support state dependents, to redistribute goods among the provinces, and to supply animals and other foodstuffs for the service of the central temples (Sharlach, 2004: 19–22). A similar rotational system is attested from the Middle Assyrian period, where the palace organized contributions to the Assur temple from surrounding provinces and royal officials were informed when obligations were not met (Pongratz-Leisten, 2012: 295). Similar contributions were ordered through royal decree in the Neo-Assyrian period (Kataja and Whiting, 1995: 71–4).

These taxes were backed by force, but they were also justified rhetorically. It was important for kings to represent themselves as humble servants of the gods, undertaking domination, extraction, conquest, and plunder as acts of piety and service rather than ambition or greed. Kings boasted of their extravagant gifts and provisions to the temple, emphasized their monumental building projects, most especially those devoted to their gods. Sumerian and Babylonian kings often portrayed themselves as "basket carriers" – that is, manual laborers engaged in monumental works of irrigation and architecture, and were depicted

Figure 4 Two stone steles showing Mesopotamian kings with work baskets (šupšikku) on their heads. On the left is Šamaš-šum-ukīn, a seventh-century king of Babylon. On the right is Assurbanipal, seventh-century king of Assyria. The symbolic nature of the basket is especially apparent in the image on the right, as the traditional royal headwear intersects with the basket in a physically impossible arrangement. Photo © The Trustees of the British Museum.

pictorially with basket, rod, and measuring rope, tools of the builders' trade (Selz, 2007: 277–8; Figure 4).

In practice, of course, the rod, rope, and basket were borne not by kings but by the various classes of laborers subordinated to the crown. In Mesopotamia, class had less to do with levels of private wealth or ownership of the means of production than with rights and obligations in relation to other persons or the state. Often, class labels do not denote membership in a discrete category so much as relative hierarchical position and relationships of authority and subordination. On a basic level, Mesopotamian social positions spanned the spectrum from "freedom, with attendant rights and duties, to full enslavement, with no duties to the state and limited rights" (Dassow, 2011: 207). Counterintuitively, perhaps, it was free citizens – the highest general social class – who bore obligations of labor and military service to the royal authority. Enslaved and servile laborers, being fully subordinated to an individual or institution, were insulated against such claims (Dassow, 2011: 207). This is the backdrop to an oft-quoted Sumerian proverb: "The palace cannot avoid the waste land. A barge cannot avoid straw. A freeborn man cannot avoid corvée work" (ETCSL 6.1.02.157).

In every period, free persons made up most of Mesopotamian society. They were referred to as *awīlu(m)*, the default term for "man," implying man in his capacity as citizen and free agent.[9] The label was not absolute, however. Only the king was an *awīlu* in relation to all others, and kings were commonly called the *awīlu* of their city (Dassow, 2011: 215). Most men who could be legitimately identified as an *awīlu* in one context could also be called "subject" (*muškenu*) in relation to the state and "slave" (*wardu*) in relation to the king personally (Dassow, 2011: 213, 2014: 291–2). For this reason, free men had an obligation to provide labor to the palace in the form of corvee (Steinkeller, 2013: 348; Dassow, 2014: 299–300). This was unremunerated labor performed for a specified amount of time per month or year, the benefits of which accrued to the state rather than the individual. As such, it took several forms. In an arrangement referred to as *ilku* in Akkadian, citizens gave a portion of their harvest to the palace in return for being granted the plot of irrigated arable land on which they worked. At other times, a certain number of labor hours were required from each citizen household to contribute to monumental building projects, including palaces, temples, walls, and major irrigation works (Steinkeller, 2013: 348–9).

The severity of corvee obligations could be a cause of strife between monarchs and their subjects. Though ruling kings seldom intimated this in their own royal inscriptions, they were happy to criticize the oppressive demands of their predecessors and boast of their own lenience. Thus, the crown was able to impose obligations of taxation and labor, but not with complete impunity. At some point, the king's rule depended on the people's consent to be governed, and the balance of rights, duties, and privileges was a locus of constant negotiation.

2.1.5 Conclusions

Mesopotamian temples – at least in their own self-representation – created a focal point around which the economic activities of city and hinterland were organized. They were the primary vector through which material sustenance, comfort, and service were administered to the gods, and so justified their gravitational pull of resources inward. They provided ideological cover for royal governance and authority, and in return the crown laundered its coerced and violent acquisitions into voluntary donations for the temple.

---

[9] As this suggests, the term *awīlum* was not only classed but also gendered. Women could be *mārāt awīlim*, "members (f.) of a household in the *awīlum*-class," when their class position was being emphasized (Roth, 2013: 267–72). Subordinate male members of awīlum households were likewise known as *mār awīlim* in such contexts.

On a material level, the temple and palace employed a variety of voluntary, persuasive, and coercive strategies to ensure that surplus production was siphoned inward to the institutions and their beneficiaries. On a symbolic level, this extraction also served to funnel resources upward to their rightful divine recipients. In this idealized model, the palace was merely instrumental – an institution mandated by heaven to facilitate and ensure the proper and consistent maintenance of the gods in the comfort to which they were accustomed. To reinforce this claim, the institutions of palace and temple had to produce appropriate etiologies for themselves, anchored in inescapable theological foundations, and it is to those that we now turn.

2.2 Mesopotamian Myths with the Labor Creation Motif

The labor creation motif finds its clearest expression in several Mesopotamian myths, beginning in the Old Babylonian period (ca. 1800–1600 BCE) and continuing through the first millennium. The gods create humans for the sole purpose of divine service, and they devise the institutions of temple and palace to organize and facilitate it. These stories take the need for labor as a given – the gods must eat and drink and live in houses, and they do not wish to do the work to provide for themselves. They create human beings to relieve all the gods from the burdensome labors of construction, irrigation, and food production. By producing such an etiology for the economic system, the elite classes push responsibility for its many problems and inequalities from themselves to an assembly of powerful and unaccountable gods. Thus, the creation accounts themselves become powerful works of political economy that naturalize and legitimize the operations of the temple and palace.

Though this common motif is often noted, few studies have delved deeply into the economic contributions of these creation myths. Rather, scholars tend to sideline them in favor of literary and theological themes. The first editors of *Atraḫasis*, for example, condescendingly note the "simple charm about the way [the poet] tells the story of the gods on strike" and treat it with much less interest than "the main theme: Enlil's desire to extirpate humanity [with a great flood] and Enki's countering this plan" (Lambert and Millard, 1969: 13). As I show, however, none of these myths can be fully understood without apprehension of their economic ideology, and seemingly unrelated events like the flood may also relate to it in unexpected ways.

2.2.1 Atraḫasis

The myth that develops the labor creation motif in the most depth and detail is known to modern scholars as *Atraḫasis*, after the human protagonist of its second and third acts.[10] The earliest and most complete manuscripts date from the late Old Babylonian period, with further fragmentary recensions attested through the mid-first millennium.[11] The best exemplars of the Old Babylonian version comprised 1,245 lines over three tablets. I cite primarily from the three most complete tablets, A, B, and C, unless otherwise noted.

Atraḫasis has attracted the most academic attention as a version of a cosmic flood story, an antecedent and close corollary to the biblical stories of Noah (Genesis 6–9), but the flood only occupies the myth's third act. The first act – covering much of the first tablet – concerns events prior to and including the creation of human beings and their social institutions. I will focus primarily on this act, with briefer consideration of the second and third.

All Hitherto Existing Society: Class Struggle in the Time of Gods

In antiquity, *Atraḫasis* was known by its opening line, *inūma Ilū Awīlum* "When Gods were Man."[12] The gods were never literally human beings, so we must look to other connotations of *awīlum* to catch the meaning. Fortunately, the opening passage elaborates:

> When gods were man
> They did forced labor; they bore the work basket[13]
> Great indeed was the work basket of the gods[14]
> The labor was heavy; the work basket excessive.
> The great Anunnaki, the Seven,
> Made the Igigi-gods bear the labor. (A i 1–6)

The gods were like men, then, in that they labored and were forced to labor. These were no ethereal, disembodied beings of pure light and spirit; they were gods with bodies, and they required food, drink, and shelter. In these early days, no other kind of being existed to do the labor, and the gods had to provide for themselves. The two terms used to describe their work, *dullu* "(forced/corvee) labor," and *šupšikku*, "work basket," recur frequently throughout the story, tracing the theme

---

[10] The first full edition of this text was Lambert and Millard (1969), which has not yet been superseded despite a raft of tablets that have been identified since its publication (see Foster (2005: 227–8) and Kvanvig (2014: 14–19). A new edition is underway at the Sources of Early Akkadian Literature project (SEAL nos. 1515–1519). Unless otherwise noted, text used comes from SEAL. Translations can be found in Dalley (2000: 1–38), Foster (2005: 227–80), and Frymer-Kensky (2006a: 5–18 and 51–66).

[11] The colophon of one OB tablet dates it to the twelfth regnal year of Ammi-ṣaduqa (=1635 BCE). For more on dating and social context, see Koppen (2010: 144–6).

[12] Some translations render this line "When gods like man," and the comparative particle is occasionally present in references and allusions to the text, such as in a letter to Assurbanipal (Lambert, 1969: 533).

[13] Others render the first two lines as a single clause, "When the gods, like man, bore the work basket."

[14] Or "the work basket of the great gods."

of labor as it wends through the narrative. *Dullu* seems to have originally meant "hardship" or "misery," gradually drifting into the semantic terrain of hard labor and eventually into work of all kinds (*CAD D*, 173–7). Šupšikku is the name of a basket used for hauling soil or bricks and so came to be used as a metonymy for the taxing menial work in which it was used (*CAD T*, 476–9). Thus, the first four lines emphasize the work and its difficulty. Only in lines five and six does the reader learn that it is not equally distributed. The seven greatest gods, the Anunna, have imposed forced labor obligations on the lower class of divine beings known as the Igigi. The chief gods of the Anunna – Anu, Enlil, and Enki – have each taken dominion over one of the three regions of the cosmos. Anu has departed for the heavens and Enki for the *Apsû* (subterranean fresh water), while Enlil has remained on earth with the Igigi.

Thus, the gods – or at least, the Igigi – are *awīlu* in its classed sense as well. Though free in some ways, they are nevertheless subordinated to the aristocratic Anunna-gods and compelled to provide them with labor. In other words, divine society is a classed society from the beginning. *Atraḫasis* does not, however, imagine the society of the gods as a straightforward analog to the human society in which it originated. Divine society is only divided into two classes: the aristocratic Anunna (together with their household personnel) and the laboring Igigi. Apparently, slavery plays no part in divine society. This dichotomic class structure was first noted by Komoroczy (1976: 29), whose analysis elucidated more of the myth's economic contributions than many before or since. The nature of the division is explicitly economic, relating to the unequal distribution of the burden of labor. It is the Igigi who perform the labor while the Anunna rest.

The specific labor relationship between the Igigi and the Anunna-gods is not one of bound subordination but of obligation. It is more akin to the corvee labor that free citizens owed to the crown, which usually involved performing work on monumental public works as well as contributing regular taxes in the form of agricultural and pastoral produce to the palace. Both *dullu* and *šupšikku* (the words for labor) were strongly – though not exclusively – associated with such work.

In this case, the Igigi must work on monumental infrastructure, measured on a divine scale. They dig the Tigris and Euphrates to irrigate the plains (A i 21–7) and pile up mountains (A i 31–3), in addition to some projects that are not well enough preserved to translate. It is toilsome work, and over the course of the years it wears them down.

Attack and Dethrone God: Labor Revolution in Divine Society

When the Igigi can take it no more. They become overburdened and resentful. Discontent turns to rage, and they band together and rise up in collective direct action against the Anunna-gods – the original patron deities of labor militancy. Scholars have often diminished the violence of their intent in translation and commentary, characterizing it as a mere work stoppage, strike, or picket line,[15] but the text is much more explicit:

> "Come, let's remove (him) from his dwelling,
> "Enlil, counsellor of the gods, the warrior,
> "Come, let's remove (him) from his dwelling!
> "Now, you all, call for battle!
> "Battle! Let's mix it up in a melee!"
> The gods heard his words,
> They put fire to their tools:
> Fire to their spades
> And their workbaskets they torched with flames.
> They picked up and went,
> To the gate of Warrior Enlil's abode.[16] (A ii 2–13)

This is no peaceful strike, as the Igigi do not only withhold their labor. Their goal is to abolish their labor obligation completely (A i 40–42) by deposing Enlil (A ii 4), and the Igigi repeatedly describe their action with the vocabulary of warfare and battle (*tuqumtam, tāḫāzum, qablam balālum*, A ii 5–6). This is an uprising, a workers' revolution aimed at ending the life and rule of Enlil.[17] Thus, Enlil reacts with true fear when his night guard and advisor wake him with news of the violent mob outside his gate, his face turning the gray-green of tamarisk (A ii 35–40). He cannot withstand the force of all the Igigi combined, and summons Anu and Enki in his alarm. Their first inclination is to identify the mob's leader and learn his demands, but in doing so, they misapprehend the economic basis of the revolt and mistake it for a political coup. When Nusku goes out as their armed emissary, the Igigi refuse to identify a leader. Nusku reports their reaction to his inquiry:

> "I shared your great [message].
> The lot [of them rejected the question, (saying)][18]
> '[Every one of us] gods has declared war,
> 'We [formed our group] in the ditch.

---

[15] (Lambert and Millard, 1969: 13; Kilmer, 1972: 162; Abusch, 1998: 363; and Frymer-Kensky (2006a: 6). Moran (1971, 52), and Kvanvig (2014: 19) are closer to the mark, characterizing it as a "revolt" and "close to a civil war," respectively, though neither elaborates the theme.

[16] The word here, *atmanu*, is used for the cellas of earthly temples (the inner chamber where the statue of the deity is housed), for temples as a whole, and for royal palaces (CAD A/2: 495–7). It seems, therefore, to refer to the deity's home.

[17] One is reminded of the militant 1960s labor organization known as the Weather Underground, whose motto was "Attack and Dethrone God." The Igigi bore this out first and literally.

[18] The reconstruction and translation of line 158 is conjectural and tentative. Millard and Lambert (1969: 50–3) do not attempt a translation of this line or its parallel in line 145. Foster (2005: 165–6) includes it as the end of Nusku's message. Frymer-Kensky (2006a: 14) includes it in the Igigi's response. My translation presumes it is an expositional break between Nusku and the Igigi's

'The excessive wo[rk basket] has killed us,
'Our forced labor [was heavy], the hardship too much!
'[Now, every] one of us gods
'Has resolved [on a battle] with Enlil.'" (A iii 43–51; cf. A iii 30–8)

This is no political coup. No charismatic leader or pretender to the throne has roused the gods to his call.[19] It is an upswell from below, the collective will of the oppressed class who speak and act as one in a leaderless movement.

Unable to behead and defuse the uprising, the chiefs of the Anunnaki must come up with another solution. Enki speaks up, as he sympathizes with the Igigi's complaint, and proposes the creation of a new creature to relieve them of their drudgery and toil.

Children of the Revolution: Humans as the New Laboring Class

Enki works together with the goddess Mami (also called Nintu and Bēlet-ilī) to create the new creatures: human beings. The humans, called alternately *lullû* and *awīlu*, are formed from clay mixed with the flesh and blood of a slaughtered god.[20] Their explicit purpose is labor – to perform the diverse labors necessary to support and nourish the material needs of the gods. In their instructions to Mami, the gods define humanity's burden as *šupšik ilim*, "the god's work basket," but also *abšānum*, "yoke," a term not used in reference to the Igigi (I 195). In this act of creation, Mami releases the Igigi from their labor obligation and places it upon humankind.

"You commanded me the task and I completed it."
"You slaughtered a god together with his reason."
"I abolished your heavy toil."
"I set your work basket on man."
"You bestowed noise (*rigmu*) on humankind."
"I removed the yoke;[21] I established a release." (A v 11–6)

Mami's language in this speech mirrors the Igigi's complaints earlier in the tablet (A i 40), as she abolishes (*nasāku* Š) their labor (*dullu*) and work basket

---

direct speech, which relates them rejecting the premise of Enlil's request for the identity of their leader.

[19] Following Moran (1970: 52), many scholars have inferred that the Igigi were roused by a god named We or We-ilu to rebel against Enlil, as he is the god slaughtered later to become the raw material for humankind. Regardless of whether he instigated the rebellion or not, the Igigi's speech here asserts collective responsibility.

[20] For further detail about Mesopotamian ideas about human nature embedded in the narrative, see Moran (1970), Abusch (1998), and Frymer-Kensky (2006a: 6–10). *Lullû* appears to be a term reserved for people who are created directly rather than born through natural reproduction (*CAD* L: 242).

[21] For *ul-la*, "yoke," some reconstruct <du->*ul-la*, "work, labor." (*CAD* A/2: 117). The sense is largely identical.

(*šupšikku*) and transfers them to humankind. This language also resembles common formulations used by kings in royal edicts of release and restoration (*CAD N/2*, 20). Her final flourish takes this resemblance further, as the word for "release" (*andurāru*) in other texts refers most often to release from slavery and the erasure of debts (*CAD A/2*, 115–7).

Enki and Mami design humanity as a self-supporting and self-reproducing labor force. As such, they also implement processes, practices, and institutions meant to guide their activity. The best preserved of these refers to reproduction, but a large gap in the text presumably also once contained descriptions of other social conventions and institutions. Unfortunately, much of this material has been lost in a long broken section (Lambert and Millard, 1969: 20; Kvanvig, 2014: 31).

Toward the end of this section, however, the humans begin to live out their dual mandate:

> Together they grasped . . .
> They made new hoes and shovels.
> They built the great canal(s)
> For the hunger of the peoples, for the nourishment of the gods. (A vii 3–6)[22]

This section clearly links the construction of canals to the production of food, although the production is framed differently in regard to its divine and human beneficiaries. The labor provides a positive good (nourishment) for the divine aristocracy but only alleviates a negative (hunger) for humanity. The humans' role as providers for the gods is primary, but it is understood that they must also support themselves in the course of dispatching their duty. They feed the gods and also assuage their own hunger. The gods must be kept in comfort; humans must only be kept alive.

The social systems and structures designed by the gods, therefore, do not serve humans as ends in themselves. Rather, they provide the parameters within which humans fulfill their created purpose of serving the gods. Thus, *Atraḫasis* provided an etiology for the regular events of Mesopotamian temples and shrines and a justification for the massive amounts of labor that went into supporting them. Within the symbolic world constructed in this narrative, the creation of humankind has altered the class composition of cosmic society. Freed from labor, the Igigi have now entered an aristocracy composed of all deities, with the Anunna still highest among them. The necessity of labor is now entirely imposed upon the human beings, a new working class with a tier of professional managers and intermediaries in the temple and palace.

---

[22] The term *bubūtu* has the meaning "hunger, famine" in addition to "sustenance," so I take this form with the adverbializing ending to mean "for (i.e., to assuage) the hunger" (*CAD B*: 301–2).

Keeping the Humans in Their Place: Disaster as a Form of Discipline

Thus ends the first act of *Atraḫasis* and its narration of human creation, from which it moves to their early tribulations and near annihilation at Enlil's hands. In the second act, Enlil arranges three catastrophes to afflict humankind: a plague (A 352–415), a drought (B i:1–ii:38), and a famine (B iii–iv). In the third, he orchestrates a cataclysmic flood to wipe them out entirely (C i:11–v:33). Each assault follows a similar pattern. Enlil complains about humanity, then conscripts the other gods to impose disaster on them. Once the calamity takes effect, Enki takes pity and feeds information to his favorite human, a man named Atraḫasis, which enables him to bring the troubles to an end.

What is it about humanity that provokes Enlil to mete out such violence? The question has long puzzled interpreters, since the text offers only the barest description. We read that the people multiplied and spread for 1,200 years, after which Enlil raises a vague and enigmatic grievance:

> [When the land extended] and the peoples multiplied
> The [land] was bellowing [like a bull].
> The god was constantly afraid at [their uproar (*ḫuburru*)].[23]
> [Enlil heard] their noise (*rigmu*)
> [and said to] the great gods,
> "The noise (*rigmu*) of mankind [has become too intense
> [with their uproar (*ḫuburru*)] I'm losing sleep." (A vii 20–26,
>   reconstructed from B 108ff)

On its face, the complaint seems minor, and Enlil's reaction excessive. He complains only that the humans are producing "noise" (*rigmu*) and "uproar" (*ḫuburru*) such that he is unable to sleep. While a minority of scholars accept Enlil's peevishness and loss of sleep as sufficient explanation for his violent response (Lambert and Millard, 1969: 9–10; Heffron, 2014; further citations in Pettinato, 1968: 173), most assume some deeper, implied problem or provocation behind the complaint.[24] This has been identified variously as Sin (Pettinato, 1968), human overpopulation (Moran, 1971: 51–61; Draffkorn-Kilmer, 1972: 167–74), or

---

[23] Line A vii:22 is ambiguous, and its translation has dramatic consequences for the interpretation of the story as a whole. The main questions concern whether *ilu/ilū* is singular or plural and the specific sense of the verb *adāru*. The writing *i-lu* could be *ilu*, "god," or *ilū* "gods." The verb *itta''adar*, on the other hand, must be a singular Gtn perfect of *adāru*. If we follow the verb and assume the subject noun is also singular, we find the anomalous reference to Enlil as simply *ilu*, "the god." The connotation of the verb *adāru* also bears upon the meaning: Does it imply fear, concern, or mere annoyance? All three are possible (CAD A/2: 103–5), but I opt for the first for reasons explained below in this section.

[24] The observation made by Michalowski (1990: 388–9) and Rubio (2013: 5) that *rigmu in creation myths represents the necessary activity and liveliness of active beings in contrast to the silence of the "time before time"* is apt at a certain level of abstraction but does not adequately address the violent responses it elicits in *Atraḫasis*.

discontent and incipient rebellion (Pettinato, 1968: 183, 197–200; Batto, 2013: 143–7). The first two have rightly fallen out of favor, as the text shows no concern for sin as a theological or moral category (Moran, 1971: 55–6) and overpopulation makes little sense as a problem within the text or for Mesopotamian society historically (Heffron, 2014: 85–6). I align most closely with the third position, interpreting the uproar as an expression of human discontent that evokes disciplinary violence from Enlil to preempt a possible uprising.

Rigmu and *ḫuburru* are both broad and general terms, as previous occurrences of *rigmu* in *Atraḫasis* illustrate. The first rigmu was made by the Igigi as they stormed Enlil's home on the night of the gods' revolution (A ii:21). Later, the gods grant *rigmu* to humankind at their creation along with the duty of labor (A V:15). This may represent noise as a neutral or even positive sign of life and activity (Michalowski, 1990: 388–9; Rubio, 2013: 5). There is some ambiguity in the current scene, therefore, but contextual cues suggest a less benign interpretation. Before Enlil's complaint, the text asserts that "the land was bellowing like a bull" (A vii:21), a sound that often signals aggression (or at least inspires caution). Later still, the same metaphor of a bellowing bull and loud noise are applied to that paradigmatic act of destruction, the flood itself (C iii 15–23). Furthermore, the trope of an overburdened and discontent humanity rousing a deity to violence appears in the introductions to several other mythological compositions, including "The Toil of Babylon" (Lambert, 2013: 301–10) and "The Slaying of Labbu" (Lambert, 2013: 361–5). In both texts, the humans' complaints result directly from their misery, which "The Toil of Babylon" explicitly attributes to the burden of *ilku* and *dullu*.[25]

It is quite reasonable, therefore, to conclude that the tumult of humankind expresses their misery under hard labor, but would this have translated into revolt if left unchecked? This we cannot know, but Enlil reacts as though it would. Enlil anticipates a threat and potential recurrence of the Igigi's uprising. That night, he had slept soundly, and had to be alerted to the danger by Kalkal and Nusku. He had felt secure in his rule and the aggression had taken him by surprise. This time, Enlil is keenly aware of the rigmu and cannot sleep through it. Perhaps his restlessness and the extremity of his violence can be read as a trauma response, hypervigilance and overreaction developed as a consequence of the fear and vulnerability he felt on the night of the gods' revolution.

---

[25] The text reads "[all the people of] Babylon were pressed into forced service (*ilku*); [small] and great bore the labor (*dullu*). [He (Marduk) heard] their uproar (*rimmāssina*), was upset in the daytime; through their complaining (*tazzimtišina*), he could not sleep in bed" (col. i 7–11; translation adapted from Lambert). *Rimmatu* has the same general breadth of meaning as *rigmu* (*CAD R*: 328–33, 358), but *tazzimtu* refers exclusively to complaints (*CAD T*: 302–4; cf. *CAD N/2*: 135–6).

Yet Enlil does not simply attack humanity out of fear or aggression but with some intention toward class protectionism and labor discipline. Enlil's interests are conditioned by his position at the apex of the aristocratic leisure class. He, Anu, and Enki sit at the top not only of divine society but also the society composed of all earthly and heavenly beings. He is free to rest because all of his needs are provided through the labor of others. From his perspective, the value of the laboring class exists as a function of its complete subordination. A troublesome laboring class is a worthless laboring class. As Tzvi Abusch (2007: 3) writes: "Humanity exists to serve the gods – for this reason it was created, but it must not burden them." Beyond this, it certainly must not threaten them. Even if their clamor had not yet transmuted into rebellion or revolution, it reminded Enlil that it could and prompted him to preclude that eventuality. Killing off some portion of the humans reminds them of their place and also decreases their strength in numbers and potential to pose a real threat to their divine overlords. He was forced to accede to the demands of the Igigi when they were laborers; he will not do so for the humans.

After drought, famine, and plague fail to curb the human tumult (due to Enki's interventions), Enlil determines to extinguish all human life with a massive flood. This time, Enki cannot avert the disaster. He is able only to save the lives of Atraḫasis and his wife among all humanity by instructing them to build a sealed boat that can weather the storm.

In a very literal sense, this final act of destruction is overkill. Enlil and the rest of the gods rely on humanity for their sustenance – indeed, created them to provide it – and in destroying the humans he also destroys their food supply. As the terrifying deluge progresses, the gods cower before its fury and become hungry and thirsty for the provisions they have just helped destroy (C iii:44'–iv:27). The section containing the flood's end is broken, but when the text resumes Atraḫasis has exited his boat and is making an offering:

> To the [four] winds [...]
> He made an offering [...]
> Providing food [...]
> [...]
> [The gods smelled] the scent
> They gathered [like flies] over the offering. (C v:30'–5')

Only Enlil is absent from the meal, and afterward Nintu makes a speech, condemning his ill-considered violence and lamenting her own complicity (C v:36'–vi:4). The gods, who had sided with Enlil originally, turn on him after witnessing the horror of the flood and feeling the hunger and thirst it produced. If "economic power is first and foremost a power to keep economic necessity at arm's length," as Bourdieu (1984: 55) has said, then Enlil has failed in his role as orchestrator of the cosmic economy. Necessity has come crashing down upon the gods with the flood. By the time Enlil arrives at the offering, enraged by Enki's resistance to his authority, he has no allies left in the assembly.

Once again Enlil must compromise with the other gods, and once again it is Enki who charts the path forward. Together, Enki and Nintu devise new means of limiting the human population. In the partially preserved final columns, they institute infertility, infant mortality, and new classes of childless temple personnel, along with other measures now lost in the breaks (C vii 1–8). In this way, humankind will continue to work and provide for their gods but will not represent a threat to divine supremacy.

Summary

The *Atraḫasis* myth expresses striking economic nuance and complexity. In the theological model of the world created by the text, all of the inequalities and injustices of the economic system are the responsibility of divine agents. It is they who devised the system and they who will punish humanity for acting outside their role. Kings and priests only serve a specific role within the system, enjoying certain benefits of course but liable to the gods for their appropriate provisions the same as everyone else.

Atraḫasis is strikingly (if not uniquely) critical of the gods, and thus (implicitly) of the power structures of human society. It casts the gods in general (and Enlil in particular) as unsympathetic figures who do not necessarily behave benevolently toward humankind or even know what is in their best interests at any given time. This tale feels no compulsion to portray its gods as good, and this is especially true of Enlil. In the end, it summarizes Enlil's flood as a *šipru lemnu*, an "evil deed," an abuse of power that is indefensible even for one of the most powerful beings in existence.

In this way, *Atraḫasis* also presents something of a parable in the negotiation of the duties of rule, particularly as it relates to threats from below. Across the narrative, Enlil models two responses to unrest among his subordinates, conditioned by his own development as a character and by the positionality of the complainants. In the first instance, the social distance that divides Enlil from the Igigi is much smaller, as they represent not only divinities but also an analog to the *awīlum* class in divine society. In this case, the threat is more imminent, more real, and more urgent, and Enlil responds with accommodation (facilitated by the ingenuity of Enki and the collaboration of Nintu). The solution to the Igigi's revolt is not punitive but generative – only one member of the rebellion must be given up to provide material for the new labor-saving technology known as humankind. The hierarchical gap between Enlil and the humans, on the other hand, is vast, and the balance of authority and obligations tilts entirely in Enlil's favor. His response errs toward positional aggression rather than accession or accommodation. In this scenario, however, Enlil models the dangers of a too punitive approach. By killing off too many of the laboring class, he endangers the flow of necessary goods to his divine nobility and thus puts his own position in jeopardy, dependent as it is on the Igigi's willingness to be governed.

At the same time as it naturalizes temple and palace extraction, *Atraḥasis* betrays ambivalence about authority and those who wield it. The myth assumes an aristocratic class perspective, but it recognizes that power is never absolute, never entirely unaccountable. Positions of authority cannot be wielded without concern for the well-being or contentedness of those in subordinate positions. As such, Enki, Nintu, and the other gods model different responses to the misuse of power by those in authority. The bulk of the divine assembly complies with Enlil's decrees – to their own eventual detriment. Nintu regrets her initial complicity and eventually challenges Enlil's behavior. Only Enki resists from the start, earning criticism and censure but being vindicated in the end.

Though Enki and Nintu show compassion for the humans and ultimately receive support from the divine assembly, they do not challenge the basic organization of human society as a machine for providing their sustenance. True freedom is never presented as a realistic or desirable fate for humankind. The purpose of human beings is still to serve the gods, and indeed it is Atraḥasis's stellar history of faithful service and piety that makes him Enki's favorite.

At its heart, then, *Atraḥasis* promotes the compassionate implementation of the classed and extractive regime of the temple and palace. It reminds the populace how fragile their existence is, and how dependent they are on the gods' toleration. It encourages docile submission to the divinely mandated system of extraction that funnels their surplus into the hands of the wealthy and powerful, while at the same time cautioning those elites against excesses of violent oppression. For the gods' human subjects, participating in the economy of divine support is a pragmatic affair more than a mark of special piety or virtue. One serves the gods not because they are good, but because they are powerful.

2.2.2 Enki and Ninmaḫ

The other primary example of a labor creation comes in a Sumerian myth known as *Enki and Ninmaḫ*. Its oldest extant tablets are roughly contemporary with *Atraḫasis*, and it was likewise copied in later periods.[26] Like *Atraḫasis*, it begins with a world of gods:

> [On that day], the day when heaven was [separated] from earth,
> [On that night], the night when heaven and earth were established
> [○○○]○○[○○]○ [○○○]
> After the Anunna gods had been born,
> After the goddesses had been taken in marriage,
> After the goddesses had been distributed through heaven and earth,
> After the goddesses had copulated(?), become pregnant and given birth,
> The gods' rations ... and ... was imposed to supply their meals.
> The great gods presided over the work, the junior gods bore the toil.
> The gods dug the rivers, with the earth from them they heaped up (Mount) Haralli.
> The gods suffered anguish, they complained about their conscription.
> (lines 1–11; translation from Lambert, 2013: 334–5)

The initial situation is similar to *Atraḫasis*, although the story proceeds with less detail and drama. The gods must produce their own food, and the greater gods oversee the lower ones who do all the work. The lower gods protest the arrangement, but they are less militant here than in *Atraḫasis*. They weep and lament but make no plan to dethrone or kill any of the greater gods.[27]

The goddess Namma takes their complaint to Enki, who is sleeping in his personal chamber (lines 12–23). His repose reinforces both his elevated social position and the freedom from labor that the subordination of the lower gods affords him.

> At that time he of great wisdom, the creator of the great gods,
> Enki, in the depths of the *Apsû*, the abyss into which no god can see,
> He lay in his bed, was sleeping, and did not rise.
> The gods gave vent to their weeping, they said, "He brought about the present grief,"
> But the sleeper was reclining and did not arise from his bed.
> Namma, the primeval mother who gave birth to the great gods,
> Brought (news of) the weeping of the gods to her son,
> "Lord, you are reclining, you are sleeping indeed,
> [..] ... ... [..] rise

---

[26] The most current editions of *Enki and Ninmaḫ* are Lambert (2013: 330–45, 498–509), Ceccarelli (2016), and ETSL 1.1.2. The incomplete state and idiosyncratic language of the myth has led to many different readings and translations. For important past translations, see Jacobsen (1987) and Klein (1997: 516–8).

[27] The beginning of Namma's speech to Enki is broken, making the behavior of the lower gods unclear. ETCSL translates "gods, your creatures, are smashing their," indicating property damage perhaps along the lines of *Atraḫasis* A ii 8–10, but without the murderous intent. Lambert (2013: 503) suggests only that they refuse to do their work.

The gods you created are complaining(?) about their set tasks.
My son, arise from your bed, with your expertise you must seek out skill.
Create a substitute for the gods so that they will be relieved of their toil." (lines 12–23; translation from Lambert, 2013: 334–7)

In this tale, it is Namma who comes up with the idea of a replacement worker to automate the gods' labors. Enki must only devise the manner of its creation and implementation. Once he designs the new creature and brings it into being with the help of various other deities, it is provided with its own means of reproduction through procreation and tasked with all the labors necessary to support the gods.

Even the more famous second half of this myth deals with labor issues, albeit in an idiosyncratic fashion.[28] After the creation of humanity, the gods celebrate with a feast. They drink to excess, and inebriated boasting turns into a competition between Enki and one of the gestational goddesses, Ninmaḫ. They dispute whose authority and abilities determine the fate (i.e., life circumstances) of individual humans. To test the matter, Ninmaḫ attempts to create people with various physical disabilities and differences, to create people for whom Enki can find no productive position in society – no means by which they might earn their own daily bread.

Each time, Enki successfully counters her attempt.[29] For the one who "could not bend his outstretched weak hands," Enki found a position as a servant of the king. The blind man he gifted music and installed as the king's chief musician. To the one with paralyzed feet, he gave the art of smithing, and made one with a cognitive disability a servant of the king. The infertile woman he placed as a weaver in the queen's household. Finally, she created a person with no genitalia, whom Enki gave a position serving before the king. The only creation that Enki cures of his disability is a man with incontinence, and ironically only this man's role in life is not specified. Presumably, he has now been returned to physical normalcy and can labor as any other person.

This part of the myth acknowledges the reality of labor differentiation – that not all humans are engaged day-to-day in the sowing, irrigation, and harvest of fields and orchards. Just as the gods have their rulers with retinues of palace

---

[28] Contra Jacobsen (1987: 151) and Klein (1997: 516), the Old Babylonian version need not have resulted from two original stories mechanically welded together. As Lambert (2013: 330–1) and Westenholz (2010: 201–2 n2) have already noted, ancient Near Eastern stories were frequently composed by rewriting and recombining pre-existing episodes. Additionally, the labor theme discussed here represents a binding thread connecting the two sections.

[29] Lines 58–78. Precise meanings for the physical conditions described in this section are difficult to determine, owing to unusual spellings and rare terminology. I have, therefore, kept my identifications rather vague. Regardless of their exact nature, the broad point that employment can be found for those with physical differences and disabilities stands. For detailed discussion with references to other literature, see Lambert (2013: 333, 507) and Ceccarelli (2016: 40–60).

personnel, so human societies have kings and queens surrounded by specialized artisans and attendants. Similarly, human bodies are not created uniformly, yet this does not release them from their obligation to labor in service of their rulers and their gods.

2.2.3 Enūma Eliš

Reflexes of the labor creation motif also appear in myths where it is far less central. A prime example is *Enūma eliš*, famous as a Babylonian creation myth but better understood as an etiology of Babylon as the greatest city in the world or a hymn to Marduk as the highest god in its pantheon.[30] It opens with an account of the gods' emergence from primeval powers and narrates an intergenerational conflict among the gods, the creation of the habitable world, and the founding of Babylon and construction of its great buildings. It concludes with a recitation of the fifty names of Marduk, each of which elevates and praises him in particular aspects.

The creation of humans is mentioned only briefly, but their purpose is consistent with the myths *Atraḫasis* and *Enki and Ninmaḫ*. When the gods conscript Marduk to battle the primeval goddess Tiamat, he agrees on the condition that they make him their king after he defeats her. The gods accept this condition, but only if he can arrange for the provisioning of their shrines (iv:2). After he slays Tiamat and defeats her army, the gods reaffirm this role (v:115) and Marduk devises an idea to provide for the gods:

> "I will bring together blood and form bone,
> I will bring into being *Lullû*, whose name shall be 'man',
> I will create *Lullû*-man[31]
> On whom the toil $^{(dullu)}$ of the gods will be laid that they may rest." (vi:5–8)

The god Ea (Enki by his Akkadian name) assists in the planning and creation of the new being, suggesting the use of blood and bone from the body of a slain god (vi:11–14). They execute Tiamat's general and consort Qingu, and form humanity from his blood:

> From his (Qingu's) blood he (Ea) created humankind,
> he imposed the toil of the gods and so freed the gods (from toil). (vi:33–4)

This important achievement is reiterated in the praises that accompany the recitation of Marduk's fifty names (vi:129–34).

---

[30] Edition: Lambert (2013: 3–144). Further discussion appears in Michalowski (1990), Seri (2006) and Lambert (2008). Translations adapted from Lambert (2013).

[31] Seri (2014: 98–9) identifies this as a quotation from *Atraḫasis*, which has an almost identical line on ms G, ii:9.

Enūma eliš thus presents the purpose of humanity in similar terms to the previous stories, but with notable differences. Though the humans are said to release the gods from their toil, that labor is never mentioned prior to this point. In consequence, no class conflict among the gods precipitates the creation of humankind. Furthermore, the class politics of divine society are much less fraught here than in the previous two narratives. Before Marduk's victory, the primary division among the gods is generational, and no mention is made of a division of labor among them.

After humans have freed the gods from agricultural labor, the gods ask Marduk how they can repay him (vi:44–54). His response: to build Babylon as his home and the location of his sanctuary (vi:55–8). The gods take up pick and shovel to build the city of Babylon with all its monuments and shrines (vi:59–69), doing the initial labor of construction before turning the maintenance of the institutions over to humankind. The mandate given to humans encapsulates a holistic summary of divine service, including reverence, invocation, obedience, and material provision. Thus, *Enūma eliš* makes the connection between the creation of humans as labor and the ongoing service of physical meals in temples and shrines crystal clear:

> Let him do on earth the same as he has done in heaven:
> Let him appoint the black-headed ones to revere him.
> The subject humans should take note and call on their gods,
> Since he commands they should heed their goddesses,
> Let food offerings (*nindabû*) be brought [for] (?) their gods and goddesses,
> May they(?) not be forgotten, may they remember their gods. (vi:112–8)

In its adaptation of the labor creation motif, *Enūma eliš* suppresses the class conflict among the gods, yet maintains the same purpose for humanity and ends up with the same labor relationship governing the ongoing support and maintenance of the gods' households.[32]

2.3 Conclusions

In these three Mesopotamian creation myths, the Igigi gods transform from a free laboring class into an aristocracy whose material needs are supplied entirely by the work of human beings. Humans are described as something between a laboring underclass and a technological innovation that provides fully automated luxury communism for divine society (Bastani, 2019). In either

---

[32] The amount of direct borrowing between these myths and its significance is debated. For one argument suggesting that Enūma eliš borrows from Atraḫasis based on general story structure and specific linguistic similarities, see Seri (2014: 98–101). She also notes that there are major differences, especially in the absence of any role for gestational and mother goddesses.

case, social stratification is justified by the nature of humankind as an inferior type of being. In *Atraḫasis* and *Enki and Ninmaḫ*, the Igigi demonstrate class solidarity and militate against their own oppression, but care little for the oppressiveness of the burden when it is laid on lesser creatures. In *Enūma Eliš*, humanity is the product of pure royal beneficence, eliminating any critique of royal power from the earlier instances of the labor creation motif. In slightly different ways, then, each of these three tales roots the institutions of temple and palace in ancient acts of divine creation and identifies their maintenance as the sole created purpose of humankind.

3 Creating Labor in Ancient Israel

From the alluvial plains of Mesopotamia, we now move westward to the hill country and coastlands of the southern Levant (Figure 5). Here, the time frame

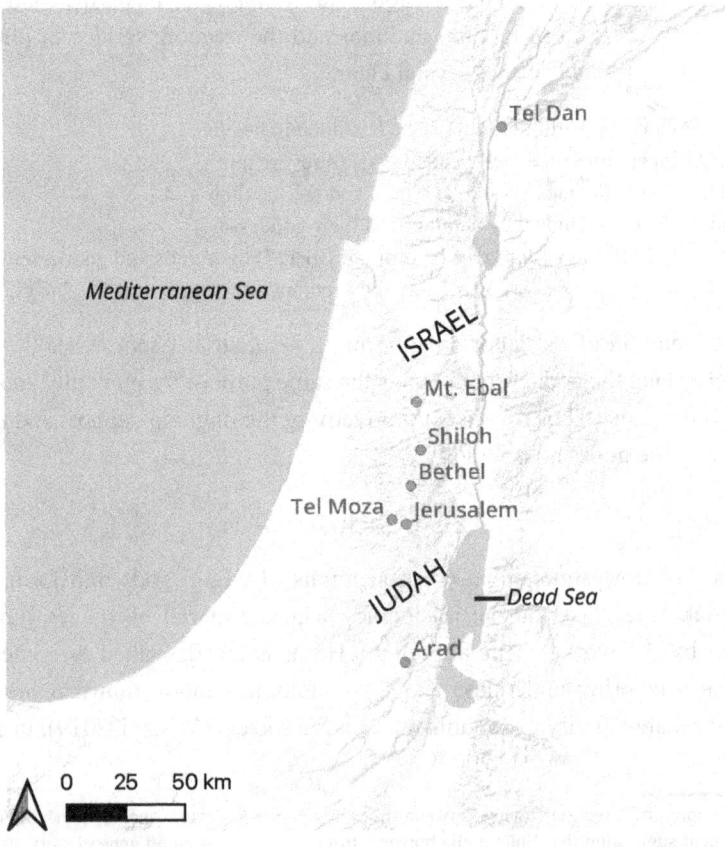

Figure 5 The Southern Levant in the Iron Age. Map by Jessie DeGrado and Eric Harvey. Basemap by ESRI.

will be compressed to Iron Age I (ca. 1200–1000 BCE), Iron Age II (ca. 1000–586 BCE), the Babylonian period (586–539 BCE), and the Persian period (539–332 BCE), since this is when worship of the deity named Yahweh emerged and came to predominate in the region. Reconstructing the southern Levantine economy and relating it to mythological texts is a significantly different task here, as the nature of the textual record is profoundly dissimilar to that of Mesopotamia. Whereas Mesopotamian texts are attested on ancient tablets – often discovered in archeological context – the majority of extant Levantine texts have been passed down within the canonical anthology known as the Hebrew Bible. Nevertheless, structural similarities in the economics of ritual in Mesopotamia and the southern Levant, combined with the closely related creation mythologies represented by *Atraḫasis* and the Garden of Eden story, make it a site for productive comparison.

The Hebrew Bible has several shortcomings as a source for southern Levantine economics. For one thing, the ephemeral texts of everyday life that are so plentiful from Mesopotamia – the receipts, inventories, accounts, distribution lists, and so on – did not tend to be included and preserved in this profoundly literary collection. For another, the theological interests of the Bible's various editors and compilers have filtered out or muted nonnormative perspectives. The Bible as a collection is far from univocal, but the diversity of its voices comprises only a subset of the full diversity of ancient southern Levantine thought. Not all residents of the southern Levant served Yahweh, for example, and many of those who did served him alongside other gods. Even among the Israelites who served Yahweh alone, disagreements were common regarding the proper locations and manner of that service. In addition, the process of collecting and compiling individual texts into their canonical forms often dissociated them from the historical context in which they were produced. This makes it difficult to know precisely when and where certain ideas and practices were espoused or contested (Uehlinger, 2015: 10–16).

To bring these general observations to bear on the current topic, the Bible contains several contrasting positions regarding divine service. Like their Mesopotamian counterparts, Israelites provided regular and occasional offerings of food to Yahweh, but biblical sources disagree on the locations from which such offerings would be accepted by the deity. Some sources limit offerings to a single monumental structure that served as Yahweh's dwelling. Others permit offerings at any location where Yahweh's worshippers choose to build an altar. Both require food offerings, but clearly these centralized and distributed service models have different economic (as well as social, ritual, and political) ramifications.

Contrasting positions appear between biblical books, but also within them. In many cases, originally separate texts were combined to form composite works. The first five books of the Bible, known collectively as the Pentateuch or Torah, form a running narrative composed from four separate sources edited together in antiquity, each of which has its own theological, ritual, and sociopolitical distinctives (Wellhausen, 1878; Baden, 2012).[33] The most extensive of these is universally believed to reflect a priestly context, and is thus referred to as the Priestly Source, or P. The non-Priestly texts of the Pentateuch derive from three other sources, labeled for scholarly convenience as the Yahwist (abbreviated J, after the German spelling), Elohist (E), and Deuteronomist (D). Each of these sources provides and origin story for ancient Israel, and each embeds collections of laws and commandments that Israelites are to follow. The laws and stories of one source, however, do not always agree with the others. P and D emphasize the importance of centralizing Yahweh's service in a single location, whereas J and E approve of service offered at locations distributed throughout the territories where Yahweh is worshipped

The differing perspectives of these sources reflect their origins in different times, places, and social locations. Their respective dates and contexts are loci of active debate, and I will not try to pin them down here but merely offer some general assumptions that guide the discussion. These texts originated at different points from Iron Age II to the Persian period, each constructing a unique mythological account of Israel's origins in the deep past. Archaeological evidence by no means confirms any of these accounts, and they are better understood as mythmaking in the sense outlined in the introduction. Each embeds its own perspective and priorities in the mythic origins of Israel, and the same can be said of their laws and commandments. Their different prescriptions for divine service and ritual probably reflect real differences in practice, but intermixed also with ideals and aspirations for perfect worship. Likewise, texts outside the Pentateuch present differing perspectives on Yahweh's service.

Despite these caveats, common logics of divine service and provisioning do emerge in the texts. Worshippers of Yahweh in the southern Levant seem to have agreed on the necessity of divine service, even if they disagreed about centralization. In the following discussion, therefore, I will examine common themes while attending to their different manifestations in the decentralized and centralizing tendencies.

---

[33] This study assumes the model of Pentateuchal formation known as the Documentary Hypothesis, even though it is now more contested than it was several decades ago. For the classic formulation, see Wellhausen (1878) and for a newer defense and renewal, see Baden (2012). For a recent state-of-the-debate volume, see Gertz, et al. (2016).

Before moving on, I must note that, owing to the Bible's past and present theological interpretation, biblical studies as a field has been both slower to recognize and quicker to resist portrayals of Yahweh as a deity with material needs and the representation of offerings as food service. In late biblical and postbiblical developments, Yahweh was dematerialized into a noncorporeal spiritual being who could have no needs at all. As such, Yahweh could not have planted a garden for his own nourishment or implemented a system of offerings to provide for his sustenance.

The point is seldom argued from the text, however. More often, it is simply assumed from the outset as a nonnegotiable constraint on interpretation. In an explicit comparison of the Garden of Eden with Mesopotamian creation myths, for example, G. Castellino writes:

> According to the narrative of Genesis, mankind is destined to cultivate the *'ădāmāh* ['soil'] (2:5) or the garden (2:15). This same purpose is assigned the creation of man in the Sumerian and Babylonian texts. ... It is here that one notices one of the really vivid differences between Genesis and the Sumero-Babylonian myths. The spiritual and monotheistic conception of God (the anthropomorphisms should not deceive us) could not permit the notion that God had need of material help from humanity. (Castellino, 1994, 91)

Remarkably, Castellino admits that the text describes Yahweh in anthropomorphic, embodied terms (like the Mesopotamian gods), but characterizes such language as a deceptive snare that can lead uncareful readers astray. Similar arguments – though perhaps with more muted polemics – recur frequently in the scholarship. More recently, Ziony Zevit has written that "since God was understood to have no needs that a garden might satisfy, its sole purpose may have been to provide aesthetic pleasure. ... But, like all gardens, God's also required hydration and cultivation, tasks within the human's competence" (Zevit, 2013: 90). Zevit, at least, acknowledges that Yahweh creates the garden for his own benefit, but cannot allow that this implies physical nourishment.

The same bias has applied to the interpretation of offerings, where scholars often dismiss culinary language as embarrassing borrowings from Israel's pagan neighbors or "linguistic fossils" from a more primitive era (Milgrom, 1990: 238). Over the past century, however, historical biblical studies and archaeological investigation have shown that Israelite religion was not wholly unique and distinct from the religions of its neighbors. Rather, Israelite religion fits within a complex of related religious systems with a mixture of shared and distinctive ideologies and practices (Scurlock, 2006b: 263–4; Uehlinger, 2015: 12). Scholars increasingly affirm that anthropomorphic language reflects Yahweh's representation as an essentially embodied being (Hamori, 2008;

Sommer, 2009; Smith, 2014, 2015; Grant, 2015; Stavrokopoulou, 2021), and a variety of biblical texts explicitly refer to offerings as food for YAHWEH (Hemmer Gudme, 2020: 176–7; and see Section 3.1.2). When Yahweh's needlessness is removed as an a priori theological constraint, the idea of these offerings as food provisions comes across clearly in the ritual and narrative texts themselves.

The following sections show how this divine food service functioned in ancient Israel, sharing a deep structural resonance with Mesopotamian practice but also exhibiting its own particularities and internal variations. Naturally, centralized and distributed service models had different economic requirements and ramifications – although many of the differences are of degree rather than kind. In any context, cult sites had to provide for their personnel as well as their deity and had to engage a variety of economic strategies to gather necessary material resources. As in Mesopotamia, these spanned the spectrum from voluntary to compelled and involved similar entanglements with ideology and state power.

3.1 Ritual and Economy in Ancient Israel

Archaeological evidence attests to several massive shifts in economic and political organization in the southern Levant from the Iron Age to the Persian period. A period of relatively dense urbanism under the Canaanite city-state system in the Bronze Age gave way to a profusion of small, distributed, and impoverished settlements in Iron I (Gilboa, 2013: 624, 641–2), followed by a reemergence of small territorial kingdoms in Iron II (Killebrew, 2013: 734–8). Conquest of the northern kingdom (Israel) by Assyrians in the late eighth century and the southern kingdom (Judah) by Babylonians in the early sixth began a centuries-long era of foreign domination, under which political, economic, and religious organizations altered dramatically.

Though the economy expanded, contracted, and shifted its energies in these periods, certain enduring throughlines can be identified. The southern Levant, even at its most urban, never matched Mesopotamia in terms of the power and density of its cities. In every period, a larger percentage of the population was consistently involved in the survival-subsistence strategy here than in Mesopotamia, which involved some degree of agricultural production and livestock raising in both its sedentary and nomadic forms (Sasson, 2010). The southern Levant also never attained the same degree of wealth or power as did Sumer, Babylonia, or Assyria. However, here too enough surplus was produced to allow the creation and growth of extractive institutions, which generally took the familiar forms of temple and palace. The following scarcely scratches the surface of southern Levantine economic structures and practices. For deeper and more comprehensive treatments, see the studies of Nam (2012), Boer (2015), Altmann (2016), and Coomber (2023).

Even so, political and economic changes had a deep impact on the structural basis of ritual and worship. The discussion of texts that follow, therefore, will show differences and contestations. Strong royalist and institutionalist voices promoted a suite of practices that differed and contradicted more antiauthoritarian streams. These disagreed on appropriate locations for Yahweh's service, the necessity and centrality of temples, and mechanisms for providing materials for ritual use and supporting religious personnel. Without lingering too much on details, it will be instructive to consider these differences in regard to the house(s), service, and servants of Yahweh.

3.1.1 Yahweh's Houses: Temples, Sanctuaries, and Shrines in Ancient Israel

Yahweh's sanctuaries – and the Jerusalem temple in particular – feature prominently in the textual record of ancient Israel. However, hints from biblical texts themselves and findings from the intensive archaeological investigation of the southern Levant show that neither this temple nor the temple system in general were uncontested in the region.

Beginning with the biblical texts, we find many that clearly articulate Yahweh's perceived desire for a house (or houses) on earth. As in Mesopotamia, the vocabulary for such structures overlaps extensively with words for human habitations: 'ōhēl (mō'ēd) "tent (of meeting)" and miškān "dwelling" for Yahweh's portable home in the wilderness and *bayit/bêt YHWH* "house (of Yahweh)" and *hêkāl "palace/temple"* for permanent buildings and complexes.[34]

Many of the Bible's most prominent voices advocate strongly for the centralization of Yahweh's service in a single, glorious abode. In the Priestly (P) texts of the Pentateuch, offerings may be served to Yahweh only in a dwelling constructed to his meticulous specifications. Within P's historical narrative, Yahweh does not give instructions for offerings and sacrifices until the dedication of the *miškan* (the mobile tent shrine where he dwelt with the Israelites after the lawgiving at Sinai) and no offerings occur prior to that point (Wright, 2015: 145–6; Feldman, 2023: 15–20). Deuteronomy and the Deuteronomistic history of Joshua through two kings (so called because it adopts a thoroughly Deuteronomic outlook) are more tolerant of offerings in multiple locations

---

[34] See Haran (1978: 13–15) for these and other terms. This is not entirely consistent. In particular, the nature of the sanctuary at Shiloh where the Ark of Yahweh resides during the period of the judges is described with both tent and permanent structure language. The major exception to this rule is the word *miqdāš*, which can refer to any divine property or sacred thing.

before there is a temple to Yahweh in Jerusalem, but thereafter condemn worship outside of it in the strongest terms.[35] This position is summarized in Deuteronomy 12:1–14, which culminates with the following command: "Take care that you do not send up your offerings at any place you see, but only at the place where Yahweh shall choose in one of your tribes – there you shall send up your offerings and there you shall do everything I am commanding you" (Deuteronomy 12:13–14). The books of Chronicles likewise identify the Jerusalem temple as the only location for acceptable service of Yahweh, relishing every bit of opulence and embellishment in Solomon's temple from the perspective of a consummate institutionalist.

These sources hold fast to the ideal of centralized service, but never present it as an actualized reality. Over and over, they mention and condemn sacred sites that fall outside their bounds of acceptable practice. These include the cult complexes set up by the kings of the Northern kingdom of Israel at Bethel and Dan (1 Kings 12:29–31; Figure 6), as well as a nebulous host of sites referred to collectively as the "high places."[36] In these places, the Israelites are charged with worshipping other deities in addition to and alongside Yahweh, including various gods referred to as the Baals and Asherahs.

Not all forms of Yahwism were preoccupied with centralizing Yahweh's service, however. The Yahwistic (J) and Elohistic (E) sources of the Pentateuch both include stories of offerings in many places, beginning with the first generations of humankind and continuing with narratives of the patriarchs Abraham, Isaac, and Jacob/Israel, who built altars after significant life experiences and presented offerings to Yahweh on them. In J's lead-up to the exodus from Egypt, Moses repeatedly asks Pharaoh for permission to lead the Israelites into the wilderness to "serve Yahweh." He insists that they must take their flocks and herds with them, because service requires offerings. In an explicit contrast with

---

[35] Note that this concerns the depiction within each source's literary world and internal chronology, not any real state of affairs. Sometimes historical material is invented whole cloth, other times it is recast at a later date to accomplish some aims in the historiographer's present. The *Miškan* as described in P would have been impossible to construct in the wilderness, and the majority of scholars view it either as an etiology for an actually existing tent shrine located at Shiloh (Haran 1978: 198–205) or an entirely fictional prefiguration of the first temple to Yahweh in Jerusalem. Even the First and Second Temples in Jerusalem cannot be reconstructed confidently, considering the lack of archaeological evidence and their incongruent representations in the books of Kings and Chronicles.

[36] High places are frequently criticized (Leviticus 26:30; 1 Kings 11:7, 12:31, 13:2, 32–3, 14:23, 15:14, 22:43; 2 Kings 12:3, 14:4, 15:4, 35, 16:4, 17:11, 21:3, 29, 32, 21:3; Jeremiah 7:31, 19:5, 32:35, 48:35; Ezekiel 6:3,6; Hosea 10:8; Amos 7:9; Psalm 78:58; 2 Chronicles 11:15, 14:3–5, 15:17, 20:33, 21:11, 28:4, 25, 33:3, 17–19), and kings are praised for tearing them down (2 Kings 18:4, 23:5–20; 2 Chronicles 17: 6, 31:1, 34:3, 22). Prior to the Jerusalem temple, they are treated with some ambivalence, however, and are not always illicit worship sites (1 Kings 3:2–4; 1 Chronicles 16:39, 21:29; 2 Chronicles 1:3,13).

Figure 6 Aerial drone photograph of the cult precinct at Tel Dan. Courtesy The Hebrew Union College, Jerusalem.

the commandment in Deuteronomy 12:13–14, the Elohistic law collection known as the Covenant Code (Exodus 20–3) even contains rules for building altars in multiple locations: "you may build for me an altar of earth and you may slaughter upon it your burnt offerings and your wellbeing offerings, your flocks and your herds, in all the places I will cause my name to be invoked. I will come to you and bless you" (Exodus 20:21–2). For J and E, then, the service of Yahweh may take place just as well outside of a temple as within, and in any number of locations. Whether they support such distributed ritual in opposition or addition to service in temples is less clear, as neither source mentions nor implies knowledge of any such structure.

Archaeology of the Iron Age southern Levant has uncovered many kinds of cult sites in and outside of city walls, aligning to some degree with biblical descriptions of cultic diversity. Detailed descriptions and typologies of these sites have been provided by Zevit (2001: 652–8) and Schmidt (2014: 266–7), among others. The concentration of grand, official temple buildings here is far lower than in neighboring regions, and even than in the same region prior to the Iron Age (Faust, 2010: 25–9, 2019: 5–11). Such structures have only been discovered at Arad (Figure 7) and Tel Moza (Faust, 2010: 28, 2019: 7–8; Koch, 2023: 191–5). On the other hand, large open-air cult sites and smaller shrines of various sizes – within and outside of city walls – have also been excavated. These include the large Iron Age 1 site at Mt. Ebal (Figure 8), the official state complex at Tel Dan, and an assortment of smaller cult rooms and niches in industrial and domestic settings (Schmitt, 2014; Koch, 2023). In short, evidence abounds for rituals of veneration and offering in the Iron Age southern Levant, but with comparatively little taking place in temples specifically (Faust, 2010: 31; Koch, 2020, 2023: 192–3).

Smaller cult areas either did not have altars or had altars too small for animal slaughter, limiting the offerings there to grain and drink (Schmitt, 2014: 274).[37] However, many do include cooking facilities, which could have been used for family and communal feasts (Schmitt, 2014: 267–9). At larger sites, deposits of faunal remains (primarily bones) imply ritual slaughter, offering, and consumption (Greer, 2013, 2019a, 2019b; Scott, 2021).

The impression that arises from a synthesis of biblical and archaeological evidence is one of diversity, ambivalence, and competition. The assortment of different kinds of cult sites and structures points toward diversity of use and practice. Biblical texts, while agreeing on the supremacy of Yahweh, espouse multiple and contradictory impulses toward centralization of his service on the one hand and dispersion on the other. In one memorable biblical scene, an Assyrian envoy attempts to exploit these divisions by pitting Yahwists who valued distributed worship against their centralizing king: "if you say to me, 'we trust YAHWEH our god' – is it not he whose high places Hezekiah destroyed?" (2 Kings 18:22).

Therefore, it may be that the perspective of the Yahwist and the Elohist would have fit well within groups that valued high places and the opportunities for communal service they represented. The Priestly and Deuteronomistic perspectives, of course, would have abhorred this outlook, but how would distributed worshippers have felt about the grand city temple, aligned and enmeshed as it was with the palace and royal power? Was it, to them, just another way of serving Yahweh, or a pernicious totalizing force bent on overtaking traditional and less authoritarian ways of serving their god?

---

[37] In this regard, note the multiple references to domestic bread and drink offerings made to the Queen of Heaven and other deities in the book of Jeremiah (Jer 7:18, 44:15–25).

Figure 7 Remains of the temple complex at Arad. Photo by Oren Rozen (CC BY-SA 4.0, via Wikimedia Commons).

Figure 8 Altar discovered at the Iron I cult site atop Mt. Ebal. Photo by Hoshvilim (license CC BY-SA 4.0, via Wikimedia Commons).

Clearly, the centralizing tendency with its emphasis on grand and imposing households for Yahweh is most similar to the Mesopotamian temple system described in Section 2.1, but this does not preclude the possibility that the distributed offering system was also conceived and undertaken as a means of providing materially for Yahweh's nourishment and pleasure – what Baruch Halpern called Yahweh's "Backyard barbecue cult" as opposed to the elegant banquets of formalized temple culture (Halpern, 1996: 303). In the next section, we shall briefly survey biblical texts concerning offerings and provisions inside and outside of temples to see how each engages with the model of divine households and service.

3.1.2 Food Service in Ancient Israel

Archaeologically, the southern Levant has produced plentiful evidence of animal slaughter and consumption in specifically cultic contexts (Greer, 2019a, 2019b; Scott, 2021). However, archaeological findings alone convey little about the conceptualization of these rituals or the deity to whom they were directed (Greer, 2019a: 6–7). For the meaning of such rituals, we must turn to the biblical texts.

Portrayals of offerings as Yahweh's food abound within the Bible's pages. These come across most clearly (though not exclusively) in temple-centric sources. A common feature in Yahweh's dwellings, for example, is an element called the "bread of the presence." These special loaves were placed regularly on a table constructed to hold them and the dishes, jugs, and utensils used in the regular offerings. As described in the Priestly texts of the Pentateuch, the table of the desert *miškan* was made of acacia wood overlaid with gold and placed on the north side of the sanctuary (Exodus 25:23–30, 26:35, 37:10–16; Leviticus 24:5–9). The bread of the presence comprised twelve large, unleavened loaves baked from two-tenths of an ephah of flour each, arranged in two rows of six on the table and accompanied by containers of frankincense. New loaves were placed on the table each Shabbat, at which point the priests were permitted to eat the ones they had just removed. Other biblical texts present variations on the practice. The book of Chronicles includes ten tables in its temple plan (2 Chronicles 4:8), and a priest at a place called Nob allows non-priests to eat of it provided they have abstained from recent sex with women (1 Samuel 21:4–6 [5–7 Heb]).

The bread of the presence is the closest biblical analog to the meals placed on stands before Mesopotamian deities,[38] but it is far from the only offering to

---

[38] In addition to the custom of displaying bread of the presence (above), commensal feasting with deities may also have been practiced in the southern Levant through the custom of the *marzēaḥ*.

Yahweh treated as food. Take the prescriptions of Numbers 28–9, a schedule of the provisions offered to Yahweh on regular days and special occasions. Academic attention tends to focus on the passage's calendrical contributions – that is, the dates of festivals, the reckoning of the year, and the way in which it organizes time. It is only one of several ritual calendars included in the Hebrew Bible, but it is the only one that specifies exact offering amounts for each day and each special occasion (cf. Exodus 23:14–7; Exodus 34:18–26; Leviticus 23; Deuteronomy 16:1–13; Ezekiel 45:18–25). The daily offering is also specified on its own in Exodus 29:38–42.

Numbers 28–9 better resemble the food schedules from Mesopotamia such as the Eanna text TU 38 discussed in Section 2.1.2, in both form and structure. These two chapters lay out the required quantities of meat, grain, oil, and drink that must be provided to Yahweh daily, on Shabbat, at the new moon, and for various annual festivals. The culinary nature of the offerings comes across clearly from the introduction, given in Yahweh's own voice:

> Command the children of Israel, saying to them 'My provision, my food for my gifts, my pleasing aroma – you shall diligently provide to me at its appointed time. (Numbers 28:2)

The first term in this list of descriptors derives from a root meaning "to be/bring near" (*qrb*), and can refer broadly to anything brought before Yahweh, procured by any means and intended for any offertory purpose. "My food" (*leḥem*) is more explicit, as it is the most common Hebrew word for bread and, by extension, for food in general. The next term (*'iššēh*), translated here as "gifts," is common in ritual prescriptions but is still not well understood (Wenham, 1987: Ch. 1, n8; Milgrom, 1990: 124, 1991: 161–2). It has traditionally been translated as "offerings by fire" due to a perceived connection with the Hebrew word for fire (*'ēš*), but it is used to refer to several offerings that are not burned, such as the bread of the presence (Leviticus 24:7) and the wine offering (Numbers 15:10).[39] It is, however, associated with food throughout the Priestly source, as in Leviticus

---

This was a meal held in private homes among the economic elites and so is condemned by the prophets as both a non-sanctioned ritual practice and an obscene misuse of wealth (Amos 6:1–7). For discussion, see DeGrado (2020).

[39] Efforts to produce a definition through etymology have been inconclusive. It has been connected variously with the root *'nš*, the same root as the words for "man" and "woman" and characterized as peacemaking between man and god and with Ugaritic *'iṯt* (a type of offering). Perhaps more promising is a relationship with Akkadian *eššešu* a type of festival attested commonly in Mesopotamian literature and associated with special offerings (cf. Linssen, 2004: 45–51). However, the *eššešu* took place each month at significant points in the lunar cycle, so if Hebrew *'iššēh* was related it would have been used more generally. Furthermore, the meaning of *eššešu* itself is obscure and it is generally left untranslated, so an etymological connection would not clarify the meaning of the Hebrew.

21:6b "they offer the gifts (*'iššēh*) of Yahweh, the food (*leḥem*) of their god" (cf. Leviticus 3:11, 16; 21:6, 21; Numbers 28:2, 24), and with the consumption of those offerings by human religious professionals (Deuteronomy 18:1; Joshua 13:14; 1 Samuel 2:28). It is most likely, therefore, that despite the uncertainty, the term relates to food or consumption, and "(food-)gifts" serves as an approximate translation.

Finally, the mention of a "pleasing aroma" (*rêaḥ hannîḥōaḥ*) hints at a fundamental difference with Mesopotamian food service – namely, that biblical texts dictate that most of Yahweh's food should be burned on the altar and sent heavenward in the form of smoke rather than served at a table. Sometimes an entire animal is burned and "turned into smoke" in this way (as in the *'ōlāh*-offering as prescribed in Leviticus 1), while at other times only a portion is burned as a pleasing aroma.

All of the regular food offerings that follow in Num 28–29 are described as *'ōlāh*-offerings.[40] The Hebrew word *'ōlāh* derives from a root meaning "to ascend, go up," and the procedure for this kind of offering, as outlined in Leviticus 1, involves burning the entire carcass of the offered animal on the alter to send the smoke heavenward. Each regular *'ōlāh* was accompanied by appropriate portions of three other foodstuffs: fine flour, top-quality oil, and alcoholic drink.[41] Daily provisions were offered at morning and dusk, each consisting of one lamb between eight days and one year old, accompanied by one-tenth ephah of fine flour, one-quarter hin of top-quality oil, and one-quarter hin of a fermented beverage. On the Sabbath, portions were doubled. On new moons and festivals, the quantities increased further and were bolstered by rams, bulls, and larger complements of grain, oil, and drink. Annual totals would have varied, as the lunisolar calendar of ancient Israel led to years with different numbers of Sabbaths and New Moons.[42] In a given year, then, the total offerings would fall in the following ranges:[43]

---

[40] The male goat given at new moons and annual festivals is called a purification offering and given without flour, oil, and drink, suggesting that it was not considered food in the same way.

[41] The ratios vary by animal and are consistent with those laid out in Numbers. 15:1–15. They are as follows. For one lamb: $1/10$ ephah flour, $1/4$ hin oil, $1/4$ hin drink. For one ram: $2/10$ ephah flour, $1/3$ hin oil, $1/3$ hin drink. For one bull: $3/10$ ephah flour, $1/2$ hin oil, $1/2$ hin drink. Correspondences of these quantities with modern measures are difficult to estimate with any precision.

[42] Much about the ancient calendar remains unclear, and I have used the modern Jewish calendar to estimate the range of New Moons and Sabbaths in the shortest and longest years, since the ancient calendar is unlikely to have exceeded this range. The shortest year contains 353 days, with twelve new moons and fifty Shabbats. The longest has 385 days with thirteen new moons and fifty-five Shabbats (Richards, 2012).

[43] Following Milgrom (1990: 243), these ranges assume that the offerings prescribed for Passover were given every day of the Festival of Unleavened Bread, as the two were originally separate observances that became fused and the Passover itself is a private offering.

- 113–115 bulls
- 36–37 rams
- 1065–1142 lambs
- 30–31 male goats
- 147 3/5–156 1/10 ephahs of flour
- 334 3/4–355 1/3 hins of oil
- 334 3/4–355 1/3 hins of alcoholic drink.

Other texts also attest to a daily meal service and schedule of provisions, though they differ on particulars (Milgrom, 1990: 487). The book of Kings describes a twice daily offering but implies that meat is only given in the morning and the grain, oil, and wine in the evening (2 Kings 16:15; and cf. 1 Kings 18:29, 36). The program in Ezekiel 40–8 (admittedly a visionary ideal that was never implemented as written) prescribes both meat and grain offerings, but only in the morning (Ezekiel 46:13–15). As in all such things, daily service likely varied from place to place and from administration to administration.

The menu in Numbers 28–9 is much more modest than that of Eanna, but it presents only the bare minimum for Yahweh's service. At the end of the schedule, it adds: "these you shall do for Yahweh at your appointed times, separate from your fulfillment of vows and freewill gifts, given as *'ōlāh* -offerings, grain-offerings, drink-offerings, or wellbeing-offerings" (Numbers 29:39).

Priests treated other kinds of offerings differently from *'ōlāh*-offerings. Where *'ōlāh*-offerings were burned whole, well-being, grain, and drink offerings were divided among multiple recipients, with Yahweh always receiving no less than the fat and blood. Yahweh's portion was always turned into smoke on the altar to send the "pleasant aroma" upward.

In other words, fire was the primary means by which Yahweh consumed food offerings, a theme that appears in narrative as well as ritual texts. A single Hebrew verb (*'ākal*) serves as the default term for eating when done by humans or animals, and consuming when done by fire. It is used in contexts where Yahweh sends (or takes the form of) fire to consume offerings directly.[44] After Moses and Aaron consecrate the *miškān* and meet Yahweh inside it for the first time, fire comes out from it and consumes offerings laid out on an altar (Leviticus 9:23–4). At the dedication of Solomon's temple, fire comes down from the sky to do the same (2 Chronicles 7:1). In a particularly evocative episode, the prophet Elijah builds an altar and wets it thoroughly to prove Yahweh's supremacy to the priests of Baal (1 Kings 18:30–8). This time, the "fire of Yahweh" comes down and eats up the animal offering, the wood, and the

---

[44] This is also true of other (angelic or ambiguous) divine beings. See Judges 6:18–21; 13:15–20.

stones and earth of the altar itself, and even "licks up" the water filling the trench around it (1 Kings 18:38). Fire is Yahweh's most common means of consumption, but one biblical story (Genesis 18) does describe the deity eating and drinking at a table with human beings. In this story, Yahweh and two companions visit Abraham and Sarah, appearing so much like humans that their hosts do not initially recognize them as divine and prepare them a meal fit for honored guests. Though his daily meals were not served like those of Mesopotamian gods, therefore, it was not foreign to the character of Yahweh to consume offerings, in human form, by divine fire, or by normal fire on an altar.

3.1.3 Food for the God, Food for the Priest

In the southern Levant as in Mesopotamia, the ritual professionals who performed divine service in temples and shrines were supported by the same offerings that satiated the god(s). As Yahweh's portions ascended to heaven as smoke and the remains burned to ash on the altar, however, no leftovers were available for redistribution to human recipients. Thus, the specific mechanisms by which priests and other sacred personnel received their meals differed in several key ways.

Biblical texts portray the local class of ritual professionals as less complex and variegated than the Mesopotamian list of standard professions. Yahweh's houses supported only two broad groups of people: the priests and the Levites. Technically, this was one group and a subgroup, since all priests were also Levites but not all Levites could be priests. The Levites were portrayed as one of the twelve tribes of Israel that had been denied a tribal territory and given instead to the sacred work of Yahweh's service. Like all such portrayals of Israelite tribes descending from single legendary ancestors, this etiology for the Levites is not consistently represented across biblical texts or supported by archaeology (Leuchter, 2017). Because they were cast as a tribe, however, groups of Levites with special duties and responsibilities were often described as smaller family units within the larger kinship group. The priesthood – that is, the office of presenting offerings to Yahweh – belonged to the descendants of Aaron (Numbers 3:10), while the descendants of Kohath were given oversight of the holy utensils and furnishings (Numbers 4:4,15–20). Levites of no special clan were responsible for the general maintenance and protection of sacred sites (Numbers 1:53, 3:5–9; Nehemiah 13:22). The internal hierarchy is communicated clearly by the Priestly source, which calls the Levites a gift to the sons of Aaron, to serve them and perform the lesser functions of the sanctuary (Numbers 18:1–7).

The Levites unique economic position was delimited by two complementary aspects of their tribal inheritance: "[T]he whole tribe of Levi shall have no territorial portion with Israel. They shall eat Yahweh's food-gifts ('iššēh) and his portion. He (Levi) shall have no portion among his brothers. Yahweh is his portion" (Deuteronomy 18:1; cf. Numbers 18:20–1; Deuteronomy 10:8–9; Joshua 18:7). Again, the etiology here is historically dubious, but it does seem to reflect the distribution of Levites throughout the region and their traditional attachment to cult sites. Their lack of a hereditary tribal territory) excluded them from large-scale agriculture or pastoralism, but inclusion in Yahweh's portion links them to the system of ritual provision.

Multiple texts state that Levites shared in food-gifts ('iššēh) offered to Yahweh (Deuteronomy 18:1; Joshua 13:14; 1 Samuel 2:28), but they did not receive their share in the form of leftovers as Mesopotamian priests did. In most cases, the victuals were apportioned prior to offering, with Yahweh's portion immolated on the altar and the priests' roasted or stewed separately. Whole burnt offerings were food for Yahweh alone, while the well-being offerings, grain offerings, and drink offerings were divided between Yahweh and his human servants. From these divided offerings, the fat and blood at least went to Yahweh, accompanied sometimes by additional cuts of meat, while the rest was divided between human parties.

Portions of offerings could be designated for the priests alone, for priests and Levites, or for these and the parties that had brought the offering to the sanctuary. Rules even governed how family members might share in the provisions (Leviticus 22:10–16; Numbers 18:8–19). Sources preserve different traditions regarding the specific portions allotted to the priests, Levites, and other parties (Greer, 2019b: 263–8), and it is likely that such practices varied between cult sites and changed over time.[45] A narrative set at the Shiloh temple implies that the custom there required priests to take a random portion pulled out of a stewing pot with a ritual fork (1 Samuel 2:13). In the Priestly prescriptions, on the other hand, the Hebrew text usually allotted the right hind limb and brisket to the priests (Leviticus 7:31–5). In Deuteronomy, it is the right hind limb plus the cheeks and diaphragm (Deuteronomy 18:3–4). Priestly regulations stipulate that priests and Levites must eat many portions in a state of ritual cleanness (Leviticus 22:4–7), practices that are supported by archaeological remains from religious sites with disproportionate representation of right limbs in locations where the ritual professionals would have dined (Greer, 2019b: 278–81; Figure 9).

---

[45] As the table in Greer (2019b: 269) shows, the situation gets even more complicated if witnesses from the Dead Sea Scrolls and ancient translations are taken into account.

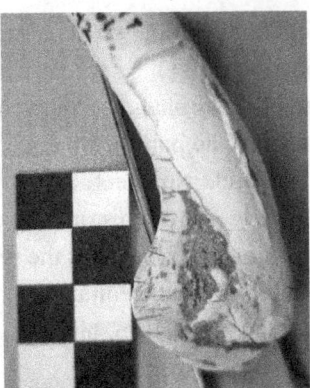

Figure 9 Sheep humerus (upper foreleg) excavated from the cult compound at Tel Dan with cut marks from butchering after slaughter. Photo courtesy Jonathan S. Greer.

Putting the pieces together, we have observed that the daily provisions offered to Yahweh according to Numbers 28–9 were all characterized as *ʿôlāh*-offerings, but also that *ʿôlāh*-offerings were not a source of food for priests and Levites. Thus, the amount of food prepared daily for the deity did not translate directly into the amount of food available to the deity's human servants, as it did in Mesopotamia. This may help to explain, if only partially, the modest scope of the daily food service in Numbers 28–9 when compared with temples in Uruk or Babylon. From a purely material perspective, the immolation of whole animals represented an extravagant destruction of precious calories. On the social and theological levels, of course, their loss would be offset by the beneficence of a happy god, but there are real limits to the quantity of resources that can be wholly surrendered even to so high a purpose. This is especially true considering the relative poverty of the southern Levant. A society cannot perpetuate a ritual system that its economy will not accommodate. To paraphrase Michael Hudson: "Offerings that can't be made, won't be made."[46] With that in mind, I turn to the strategies and means that sacred institutions used to acquire the resources they needed to sustain their activities and their personnel.

3.1.4 Ritual and the Economy

Since the Levites held no tribal territory, several lists suggest they were granted towns distributed throughout the other tribes' lands (Numbers 35:1–8; Joshua 21; 1 Chronicles 6). This may represent a utopian ideal more than any real state

---

[46] The original is "debts that can't be paid, won't be paid" (Hudson, 2018).

of affairs, as there were supposed to be forty-eight such towns (four in each tribal territory), each within a perfect 2,000-cubit square of land for their livestock (ca. 80 ha.). Nevertheless, the basic notion that they did not participate in the survival subsistence economy through staple production probably stands. Instead, the texts present a variety of economic means used to ensure an adequate supply of animal, grain, and beverage provisions for the food service, other rituals, and priests' livelihoods (Koch, 2020: 342–4). Naturally, these looked different for centralized and decentralized worship practices, as each interacted differently with local communal political formations and with the state. The following provides a brief survey of practices that could apply in either context.

Distinctions must be made between vectors that were voluntary, upheld through social pressure, and coerced or forced. In the first category, biblical texts delineate options for individual Israelites to give gifts out of their own free will and in thanksgiving for good fortune (Leviticus 7:12–15, 22:29; Amos 4:5; Psalms 50:14, 56:13, 107:22, 116:17; 2 Chronicles 29:31, 33:16). In addition, many texts reference the practice of making a vow to Yahweh, promising a donation of some kind pending the positive outcome of an uncertain situation, such as infertility or a military venture. These could range in value based on the person's means, from grain and small birds to large cattle and houses. Vows could even be made with human beings, who would then be redeemed for money (Leviticus 27:1–8) or bound to temple service (1 Samuel 1–2).

Levantine cult sites may also have profited from transactions similar to the Old Babylonian temple loans. Leviticus 27:14–25 outlines the procedures and prices for buying back items that had been previously designated as sacred donations, but it does not discuss motivations for their initial donation. It may be, therefore, that they were given as votive, freewill, or thanksgiving gifts and repurchased or traded in exchange for money that could later be repaid.

Other donations were framed as obligatory. Yahweh claimed the first portion from every harvest, including raw produce (Leviticus 23:9–14; Deuteronomy 26:1–11) and the first loaf from each grain harvest (Numbers 15:17–25). Israelites were also commanded to surrender every firstborn male to Yahweh (Exodus 13:12–15; Numbers 18:15–18; Nehemiah 10:36).[47] This requirement

---

[47] The pronounced preference for offering young male animals aligns well with standard practices of culling for herd health. Pastoralists keep only the minimum number of males necessary for breeding, since they produce no milk and have a generally aggressive disposition. In British Mandatory Palestine, which is often used as a rough anthropological parallel to ancient Israel, livestock censuses found that herds were composed of over 50 percent adult females, 20–25 percent young females, 10–15 percent young males, and only 3–5 percent adult males, and these ratios match the age distribution of animal remains in many Israelite archaeological sites (Sasson, 2010: 40–2, 55–8, 112–13).

applied to clean animals, unclean animals, and humans alike. Clean animals were kept, offered to Yahweh, and eaten, while unclean animals and children were purchased back (or "redeemed") for a specified sum of money. A tithe of all produce also went to the Levites specifically, which could be delivered in the form of staples or their monetary equivalent (Numbers 18:21–32; Deuteronomy 14:22–9, 26:12–15; Nehemiah 10:37–9). Thus, several practices could yield both in-kind and monetary contributions.

Opportunities to collect these donations at scale occurred at the three annual pilgrimage festivals, which coincided with harvest times for major crops: Passover/Unleavened Bread for the barley harvest, Weeks for wheat, and Ingathering/Booths for wine and olives (Exodus 23:14–18, 34:18–26; Deuteronomy 16:1–17; see Farber, 2019). All Israelite men were to congregate at a sacred site for each festival, and the commandments stipulate that "no one shall come before me (Yahweh) empty-handed" (Exodus 23:14–15; Exodus 34:20; Deuteronomy 16:16). Acceptable pilgrimage locations varied, of course, as did the nature of the offerings. The Elohistic laws in Exodus 23, which permit distributed service, mention only contributions of produce and livestock. Deuteronomy, with its centralizing impulse, recognizes that transporting bulk goods to the one authorized sanctuary may represent a hardship to those who live far away, and allows them to sell their goods and bring the proceeds instead. These donations – whether goods or money – supplied the festival offerings for Yahweh, furnished grand communal feasts for the assembled worshippers, and filled the storehouses of the cult site until the next gathering.

Royal administrations also supported temples and cult sites directly. Narratives describe kings as patrons of Yahweh (and other gods of the southern Levant, depending on their disposition), who built, destroyed, and renovated cult sites (1 Kings 5–8; 2 Kings 22:4–7; 2 Chronicles 2–7) and provided grandiose offerings as signals of piety and power (1 Kings 8:62–5; 2 Chronicles 7:1–8). The most celebrated of these was the first temple to Yahweh in Jerusalem, credited to Solomon in the late tenth century and renovated by Josiah in the seventh. These gifts and projects were furnished by all of the tricks of royal power – corvee and conscription (1 Kings 9:13–23; 2 Chronicles 2:1–2, 17–18), taxation (Ezekiel 45:13–16), trade (1 Kings 9:25–28), and plunder (1 Samuel 17:53; 2 Kings 7:16).

The burden of royal extraction and expropriation weighed heavily on rural producers, and several biblical texts express disapproval with its excesses (Yee, 2017: 828–31). When the Israelites first ask for a king to rule over them, the prophet Samuel warned them about the voracious appetite of royal expropriation: their fields, vineyards, and orchards, sons, daughters, slaves, work animals, and livestock would all be claimed and seized by the king for his own purposes and benefit (1 Samuel 8:10–18). Ironically, Samuel excoriated royal oppression without acknowledging the economic weight of divine service itself or the oppressive corruption of his sons that had motivated the people's request for a king in the first place. In general, biblical texts take a more critical view of the extractive activities of the palace and nobles, while glossing over those of the temple regime. Of course, in many periods the two were deeply entangled with one another, but it is almost always the secular authorities that find themselves the targets of prophetic critique.

The first temple in Jerusalem was destroyed by the Babylonian army in 587/586 BCE and the elite classes were exiled to Babylonia. The temple was not rebuilt until Babylon fell to the Achaemenid Persians in 539 BCE and exiles were permitted to return home. Sometime during the exile, a prophetic figure wrote down a visionary program for Israel's restoration, which is now contained in Ezekiel 40–8. This program would have cemented state control over the Jerusalem temple while explicitly attempting to limit its oppressive potential. Providing the materials for regular scheduled offerings would rest on a royal figure referred to as "the prince," whose stock would be furnished by a percentage tax on all the people of Israel. In this way, "all the people will join together to offer the offerings through the prince" (Ezekiel 45:16). The size of the tax is specified to avoid the oppressive overreach of past kings: 1/16 part of the wheat and barley harvest, 1/100 part of the olive oil, and one sheep or goat from every flock of 200 (Ezekiel 45:13–16).[48]

This vision was never realized, and in the actual context of Achaemenid imperial rule, temple accounts may have been kept more separate from the state. The book of Nehemiah recounts a pledge – a voluntary compact pertaining to the direct support of the rebuilt Second Temple – made by a group of people who describe themselves as adherents to the "law (Torah) of Yahweh" (Nehemiah 10:32–9). The pledge includes a list of voluntary donations for all aspects of "the service of the house of our god" (Nehemiah 10:33), including an annual monetary contribution of one-third shekel and supplies of wood for the altar on top of the firstfruits and firstborn offerings already discussed. The economic organization and political entanglements of the temple experienced further changes and developments through the Hellenistic (332–163 BCE), Hasmonean (163–63 BCE), and Roman periods until the destruction of the Second Temple by Rome in 70 CE. These cannot be covered here, but this brief discussion should serve to illustrate the many processes that mobilized resources for use in the sacred work of divine service in the southern Levant.

---

[48] Amounts of other products, such as bovines, beer, and wine, are not specified.

3.1.5 Conclusions

As in Mesopotamia, southern Levantine sources from the Hebrew Bible portray divine service as an imperative for humankind. Human beings were required to serve regular provisions to the deity in addition to all of the other sacred duties and rituals they were obligated or permitted to perform. In contrast to Mesopotamia's broad adoption of the divine household model, though, the multiple voices of biblical texts betray a deep split regarding the appropriate location and manner of divine service. Did meals have to be served in a grand dwelling, a house for Yahweh, or could they be sent heavenward as smoke from altars across the land? Local altars and central temples alike had to support their personnel as well as supply their rituals, with a shared suite of economic strategies to engage. The burdens and benefits of divine service could change in relation to religious leadership and the demands of the state.

One could imagine, for example, that small communities used the three harvest festivals to gather at local shrines, feast together, and store their produce for use in divine service and common use. This kinship-based allocatory form would invite the intangible benefits of a happy deity while maintaining community control over material surpluses they produced. As the corruption and greed of Samuel's sons (and the sons of Eli before them) shows, however, even local ritual professionals could abuse their sacred and economic power. This only intensified when divine service was consolidated in a central location and bound up with royal power. The monumental construction efforts of Solomon were only enabled by corvee labor and broad taxation, and the oppressive and exploitative demands of Israel's monarchs gave prophets frequent cause for condemnation.

Across these divides, the ideology of divine service remained alive and well. It shows up in both decentralized and centralizing texts, with different economic implications. Both tendencies could plausibly be bolstered by the labor creation motif, but the only example of the motif appears in a decentralized source: the Yahwist's story of the Garden of Eden. We now turn to a discussion of this story and its relation to the Levantine ideology of divine service.

3.2 Laborers in Yahweh's Garden

Like their neighbors in Mesopotamia, the inhabitants of the Iron Age southern Levant produced several and varied accounts of the world's origins. In Genesis 1–11, not one but two stories appear woven together into a running narrative (Figure 10). The Bible's opening line, "When God began to create the heavens and the earth" (Genesis 1:1) is the start of creation according to the Priestly source (P), while "On the day when Yahweh God made earth and heaven" (Genesis 2:4b) introduces creation according to the Yahwist (J). Both of these

Figure 10 The Dead Sea Scroll manuscript 4Q2 (4QGenb), which includes text from Genesis chapters 1–2 (main assembly), and 4 (left fragment). Courtesy of The Leon Levy Dead Sea Scrolls Digital Library, IAA. Photo: Shai Halevi.

continue through Genesis 11 in alternating passages and verses, but only J's version conveys the labor creation motif. J's creation and primeval history include the story of the Garden of Eden (Genesis 2:4b–3:26), Cain and Abel (4:1–26), one version of the life of Noah and the great flood (5:29; 6:1–8; 7:1–5, 10, 12, 16b–17a, 22–3; 8:6–12, 20–2; 9:18–27), and the Tower of Babel/Babylon (11:1–9), with perhaps a few other verses and verse fragments besides.

The Yahwist's primeval history is densely packed with themes and etiologies, and any reading that reduces it to a single meaning or message will fail to capture it completely (Greenstein, 2002: 234). However, millennia of Jewish and Christian interpretation have often favored theological and anthropological themes like good, evil, sin, mortality, sex, and gender (Zevit, 2013: 1–13; Levine and Brettler, 2020: 101–34) and have generally neglected the role of labor relations and class politics to the development of the plot.

That is not to say that labor has been ignored entirely. In her rereading of Gen. 2–3 in light of the archaeology of ancient Israelite household economies, Carol Meyers challenged patriarchal readings of the Garden Story that emphasized gender hierarchy above all else in favor of one that balanced reproductive politics with women's shared participation in agricultural and domestic labor (Meyers, 1988, 2012). Gale Yee analyzed the class and gender dynamics at play in the

Garden of Eden story, demonstrating its patriarchal upper-class orientation, but with more attention to royal extraction than the economics of ritual (Yee, 1999). Edward Greenstein argued that the humans were created to help "give God a hand" running his private garden and even discussed the creator's fear of the creation's escape and rebellion (Greenstein, 2002: 231–4). Perhaps most closely to my approach, Bruce Wells has recently elucidated the portrayal of human beings as bound laborers in the Garden of Eden through comparisons with records concerning Neo-Babylonian temple oblates (Wells, 2020: 648–9, 2023). None of these studies, however, has exhausted the economic themes of the Garden Story or drawn out all its implications as a work of political economy within the common theological and literary environment of the ancient Middle East.

The themes of labor relations and class politics represent crucial points of comparison with the Mesopotamian myths in Section 2.2 as a point of alignment rather than contrast. Comparisons with Mesopotamian myths, where they have engaged economic themes, have tended to adopt the flawed interpretation that identifies overpopulation as the primary concern of *Atraḥasis* (Section 2.2; cf. Meyers, 2012: 101). The Garden Story can be best understood when it is read together with the Mesopotamian stories in two key ways: (1) that the garden was planted to provision Yahweh and (2) that human beings were created to perform the necessary labor of cultivation. In this way, the Garden Story, like its Mesopotamian parallels, aligns itself with and justifies the practices of divine food service described in the previous section. To illustrate these points, I will first offer a reading of the Garden Story that presumes them to be true and then discuss a few specific issues in the reading.

3.2.1 A Labor Reading of the Garden of Eden

The Yahwist's primeval history, like *Atraḥasis* and *Enki and Ninmaḫ*, is no creation story in an absolute or cosmic sense. It is, rather, a story of origins from when the world was young. It opens on a world already rough-hewn, shaped but devoid of life, and the narrative relates how it has come to be filled with its many living things and institutions.

The opening of the Garden Story directly parallels the Mesopotamian myths discussed in Section 2.2,[49] beginning "when" before describing an early, primeval world:

> When Yahweh Elohim made earth and heavens, before there were any wild plants on the earth and before any cereal grasses had sprouted, because

---

[49] Like Akkadian *inūma/enūma*, Hebrew *běyôm* is a compound word created by combining a preposition meaning "in" with the word for "day," which can generally mean "when" or refer to a particular day.

Yahweh Elohim had not sent rain on the earth and there was no human to work the ground. (Genesis 2:4b–5)

The presentation is curious, since it explains the lack of vegetation through the absence of its preconditions. No wild plants populate the uncultivated land because Yahweh has not yet sent rain, and no crops fill the fields because there are no humans to work them. The implication is that crop cultivation is an existing problem waiting to be solved – that is, that Yahweh desires crops but must arrange means for their production. Thus, agriculture is not first for humanity's benefit but for Yahweh's. Within the common ancient Near Eastern framework that gods need food and drink, agriculture exists first and foremost to provide for the gods' diet.

No mention is made of Yahweh laboring or tasking other deities with his labor. Instead, he makes a human to meet the need from the first (Genesis 2:6–7). The human ('ādam) is intimately connected with the earth ('ǎdāmāh) – sculpted from it, named after it, and destined to work it and to bring forth its bounty.

Next, Yahweh plants a garden in the place called Eden (Genesis 2:8). He sprouts therein every good and desirable tree, with the Tree of Life and the Tree of the Knowledge of Good and Bad in its center (2:9).[50] In a lengthy excursus, the narrative mentions a river that waters the garden before splitting into four and spreading throughout the rest of the earth. Thus, just like the minor gods in the Mesopotamian stories laid the groundwork for human agriculture by creating the landscape and digging enormous rivers to irrigate it, so here Yahweh makes and plants the garden and arranges for its irrigation.

Once the garden has been created, Yahweh settles the human within it and instructs him in his new role:

> Yahweh took the human and situated him in the garden of Eden to work it and to keep it.
> Then Yahweh Elohim commanded the human thus: "From every tree in the garden you are permitted to eat, but from the Tree of the Knowledge of Good and Bad you shall not eat any part, for on the day you eat from it you shall surely die." (Genesis 2:15–17)

The twofold mandate to work ('ābad) and keep (šāmar) the garden closes the loop opened in 2:5 – where crop cultivation was impeded by a lack of workers. Wells (2023) has shown how Yahweh's garden resembles gardens

---

[50] I avoid the traditional rendering "Tree of the Knowledge of Good and Evil," as it strikes a decidedly moralistic tone and implies too strong a connection with Sin ((and thus, with the doctrine of the Fall). I side with a more general interpretation, in which the good and the bad represent a merism that encompasses the full range of all knowledge (Meyers, 2012: 78–9) – that is, with striking thematic resonance, "all the good things and the bad things that may be" (Salt-N-Pepa, 1991).

owned and administered by Neo-Babylonian temples, and how the position of the human mirrors that of the temple dedicants (*širku*) who worked them. Yahweh's statement here reads much like administrative orders from such gardens, wherein supervisors delineate the duties and privileges of the laborers and set punishments for infractions. In the same way, Yahweh tasks the human with tending his garden, and permits the usufruct of most of its produce in the course of dispatching this duty. Only the fruit of the Tree of the Knowledge of Good and Bad is prohibited, although no reason is yet given. Apparently, this tree produces fruit that is only suitable for divine beings, not children of earth.

After this, Yahweh observes that it is not good for the human to be alone (Genesis 2:18). Though Yahweh may be concerned for the human's social life to some degree, it is just as likely that the problem is with overwork and a need to share the load (Greenstein, 2002: 236). Yahweh does not set about making a friend, companion, or lover for the human, but a "helper as his partner" (*'ēzer kĕnegdô*). This does not imply hierarchy or subordination, as Yahweh himself is often called an *'ēzer*. Rather, it connotes an appropriate co-laborer – a being capable of participating with the first human in the shared work of the garden.[51] For this reason, Yahweh's first attempts fail. He sculpts all manner of beasts and birds from the earth, but none has strength, intelligence, and opposable thumbs in appropriate portions to match the human. Yahweh finally creates a fitting counterpart in the form of a woman, created not from the earth but from the first human's own body.[52] She is made of the same substance as the other human, who now may be called a man, and she has the same basic form. She is a proper coworker for the man in his horticultural work, better suited to it than the beasts and the birds (Greenstein, 2002: 235–7). In this reading, that which has been considered primary – the woman's opposite role to the man in sexual reproduction and the gendered division of labor and caregiving – takes a back seat to her ability to share their common purpose of agricultural labor.

As chapter two closes, the man and the woman represent a workforce of two. They live together in the garden, unclothed and without shame. We do not know how long they served in this role, however, as the next scene introduces a new problem. A clever talking snake convinces the woman to eat from the Tree of the Knowledge of Good and Bad, and the man follows suit. In their exchange

---

[51] The literature on this passage and the term *'ēzer kĕnegdô* are vast. For discussion, alternate etymologies, and translation options, see Meyers (2012: 73–5) and Zevit (2013: 127–37).

[52] The common rendering of Hebrew *ṣēla'* as "rib" is possible but by no means certain. Many attempts at identification have been made from the Mishnah to the modern era, from rib to tail to buttocks to baculum. For a discussion of historical explanations and an argument for the latter position, see Zevit (2013: 140–51).

leading up to her eating, the snake tells her she will *not* die from eating the fruit, but that her eyes will be opened instead. When the woman inspects the tree herself, she observes that it is "good for eating, pleasant to the eyes, and desirable for instruction" (Genesis 3:6).

Indeed, once the humans eat from the fruit, "their eyes were opened and they knew that they were naked" (Genesis 3:7). Initially, it does not state that the eating caused them to know good and bad, but Yahweh says as much later (3:22). Rather, the immediate consequence is a recognition of their nakedness and the desire to hide it, indicating that this represents at least some significant element of their newfound knowledge.

When Yahweh comes to meet with them in the evening (the time for one of the daily food offerings [Wells, 2023]), he discovers their transgression and new state of knowledge. He imposes penalties upon each of the parties involved (Genesis 3:14–19). He curses the snake to crawl on its belly, to eat dust, and to be in perpetual conflict with the woman and her offspring. He afflicts the woman with toil, many pregnancies, and sexual subordination.[53] He curses the ground on which the man will work, forcing him to battle thorns and thistles to grow grain for his bread. It is only now that gender entails the division, rather than the sharing of labor. The labor for which both man and woman were created Yahweh makes more difficult, more painful, and less rewarding. No more will humans enjoy the easy gig that was tending to Yahweh's garden. Now they shall toil to grow food from poor soil until they return to the dust from which they came.

Notably, nobody dies (yet). Yahweh had attached a death penalty to his original command but decides to enact a different punishment in an address to unidentified interlocutors.

> Yahweh said "Look, the human is like one of us, knowing good and bad. Now he must not reach out his hand and take also from the Tree of Life and eat and live forever!" So, Yahweh Elohim sent him out from the Garden of Eden to work the ground from which he was taken. (Genesis 3:22–3)

According to this statement, gaining the knowledge of good and bad brought the human(s) one step closer to godhood, implying that eternal life would bring them closer still (Wells, 2020: 655). Presumably, the acquisition of eternal life alone would not have disqualified them from their service in the garden, since the tree was not itself forbidden, but the increase in wisdom engendered by the Tree of Knowledge creates an anxiety in Yahweh and his companions. There is no sense in the narrative that their fear is feigned or unfounded – the possibility

---

[53] As argued by Meyers (2012: 101–2), this pronouncement concerns the woman's role as necessary agricultural and domestic laborer and as bearer of children.

that the humans could become gods (or like gods) is real and it is something Yahweh would prefer to avoid.

In this sense, the expulsion can also be understood as labor discipline. If the humans become (like) gods, they would no longer classify as workers. Like the Igigi in Mesopotamia, they would leave the working class and enter the ranks of the divine aristocracy. If they were killed, as Yahweh had threatened, they would no longer be able to supply agricultural labor or products. Expulsion, on the other hand, maintains both humans' subservient position and their ability to provide labor and food offerings to the deity, although it makes their task more onerous.

Following their expulsion, Adam and Eve bear two children who continue their obligation to provide food for Yahweh in the world outside the garden (Genesis 4:1–4). Cain tends crops like his parents while Abel raises animals. Abel's occupation bears particular notice, since Yahweh originally gave humans permission only to eat plants (Genesis 2:16) and the permissibility of meat consumption is unclear. It may be, then, that Abel tended the flocks primarily for Yahweh's food, only taking wool and dairy for his own and the other humans' benefit.[54] He knows which meat offerings to bring to Yahweh – the firstborns and the fat portions – and apparently knows how to slaughter, butcher, and prepare them appropriately. This suggests a continuity of practice with his parents, who had provided for Yahweh in the garden.

After several generations, Yahweh, like Enlil, gets angry with the humans he has created and vows to destroy them with a flood. In this case, it is not noise, overpopulation, or incipient revolution that infuriates the deity, but some unspecified evil that occupies humans' every thought (Genesis 6:5–6). The forbidden fruit had granted knowledge of good *and* bad things, but it seems the humans were exploring one end of the spectrum to the exclusion of the other.

As in *Atraḫasis*, only one family survives the flood. Yahweh preserves the life of his favorite, Noah, by ordering him to ride out the flood in a giant boat. Unlike the Mesopotamian gods, who do not anticipate the disruption to their food supply that the flood will cause, Yahweh plans ahead for his ongoing provisions. He instructs Noah to bring one breeding pair each of all unclean animals, but seven breeding pairs of every clean kind (i.e., those that are suitable for divine offerings;

---

[54] Dietary permissions and restrictions are more ambiguous in the Yahwistic source than the Priestly. In P, Yahweh commands all creatures to be vegetarian before the flood (Genesis 1:29–30) and only grants permission to eat meat afterward (Genesis 9:1–6). In J, Yahweh instructs the humans to eat plants from the garden (Genesis 2:8–9) and never explicitly changes the policy. Neither source mentions dairy, likely because it did not require killing a live being and was thus presumed permissible. It is also worth noting that Yahweh's invitation to eat of the trees in the garden was made before animals existed. It may be, therefore, that J's humans simply started eating meat on their own prerogative without earning censure from Yahweh.

Genesis 7:2–3). He does not say why Noah should bring these animals, but Noah takes the hint and offers meat to Yahweh immediately after the flood subsides:

> Then Noah built an altar to Yahweh. He took from all the clean animals and all the clean birds and sent them up as ʽōlāh-offerings on the altar.
> Yahweh smelled the pleasing aroma (rēyaḥ niḥōaḥ) and Yahweh said to himself "No more will I curse the ground on account of humankind, though every machination of the human heart is bad from their youth, and never again will I destroy all life, as I have done." (Genesis 8:20–21)

Implicitly, the humans' continued existence is predicated on Noah's willingness to fulfill his obligation for service. Only after the offering does Yahweh promise clemency. His opinion of humans does not change, but he permits them to survive and multiply and participate in the eternal cycle of seasons and years (Genesis 8:22) because they supply his regular provisions.

By removing the curse he had placed on the ground (Genesis 3:18), Yahweh makes the people's lives a little easier. This ties back also to Noah's birth narrative, where his father names him Noah (similar to Hebrew for "rest") because he will "give us rest from our works, from the toil of our hands, from the ground that Yahweh cursed" (Genesis 5:29). By prioritizing Yahweh's food service, Noah has earned some respite from humanity's curse. After the flood, he manufactures another source of relief, though this one bears mixed results. Noah becomes a "man of the earth" and plants the first vineyard (Genesis 9:20). Wine, of course, offers some respite from a life of physical labor, but it also brings the consequences of drunkenness, which manifest immediately in Noah's case (Genesis 9:21–7). Neither does it remove the burden of agricultural labor, meaning that in Noah's day also "work [was] the curse of the drinking classes."[55]

Finally, the Tower of Babylon presents yet one more explicit effort by Yahweh to disempower humanity (Greenstein, 2002: 238). This time, the labor that draws his ire is that of construction, not subsistence. As the humans build a tower to the heavens from fired bricks, Yahweh considers the consequences of such an endeavor:

> Yahweh said "Look, they are one people, all of them with one language. This is (only) the beginning of what they will do – now nothing they intend to do will be impossible for them." (Genesis 11:6)

This speech resembles – thematically and even grammatically – the anxious exclamation of Genesis 3:22.[56] In each situation, Yahweh expresses sincere

---

[55] A witticism that predates but is apocryphally attributed to Oscar Wilde.
[56] Each opens with the attention-directing particle hēn, describes an event, then describes a possible but undesirable consequence beginning with wĕʽatāh "and now." Finally, Yahweh initiates an action to preempt the possibility.

apprehension at the capacity of humankind to exceed their prescribed role and escape their obligations. To stymie their common purpose, he diversifies their speech into mutually unintelligible languages. Like expulsion from the garden and mortality, this change places an ongoing check on the capability of human beings to act collectively and rise above their station. Unlike in *Atraḥasis*, there is no additional imposition of morbidity here, as Yahweh had already decreed a limitation on human lifespans in Genesis 6:3, after which they can be observed to gradually decrease in the genealogical lists.

3.2.2 Discussion of Issues in the Labor Reading

This reading may provoke objections on several counts, most profoundly the portrayal of Yahweh as a deity who requires sustenance and the creation of humanity primarily to meet that need. The first point has been addressed in the discussion of food service (Section 3.1.2). I shall discuss the second here.

The point that humans in the Garden Story were created to meet a need rather than as ends in themselves becomes clear through comparison to the Priestly creation story in Gen. 1:1–2:4b. P identifies humankind as the culmination and capstone of creation, made in God's image and likeness to solve no open problem. Their mandate includes no service requirement; rather, they are commanded to "[b]e fruitful and multiply and fill the earth and subdue it and have dominion over the fish of the sea and over the birds of the air and over every living thing that moves upon the earth." (Genesis 1:28). Later, the Priestly source will introduce the obligation of divine service necessary to maintain a harmonious relationship between Yahweh and humankind, but here the implication is that human beings oversee and enjoy the earth and all that is in it as they spread across the land.

The general posture of creation could scarcely be more different between the two chapters. In Genesis 1, incompleteness is expressed at no point in the sequence of creation. Each new stage in creation is built upon the foundation of those that came before, but never *toward* some pre-ordained state, and especially not to fill some acknowledged lack. There is no sense, at the end of each day of creation, that it *needs* something to follow to complete it. Even the blessing and mandate for humankind to subdue and rule the earth and all that is in it arises unexpectedly, as no prior indication had been given that the birds and animals needed anyone to rule them.

The Garden Story, on the other hand, constantly relates new creations to the problems they are meant to solve. Yahweh creates a garden and a human to address the absence of agriculture, but this creates the new problem of a solitary and overworked human. Yahweh attempts (unsuccessfully) to ameliorate the burden by creating animals and then (successfully) by creating a woman. A new problem arises when the humans eat from the forbidden tree, with the potential for more trouble if they eat from the Tree of Life. Yahweh addresses this by expelling them from the garden and making them miserable, but this leads to strife, murder, and the growth of a general tendency toward evil in the human heart. Yahweh responds with the flood, preserving only one human family with enough supplies to restart the schedule of provisions. Much like the efforts of the Mesopotamian gods to solve their labor problems, each solution both addresses an existing problem and creates a new one that must be solved in turn.

Thus, the humans were created to do the agricultural work that needed doing, and this was not primarily for themselves. Even the wording of Yahweh's administrative order suggests their subordinate position. The mandate to work (*'ābad*) and to keep (*šāmar*) the garden carries strongly hierarchical connotations. In the vast majority of attestations, *'ābad* especially refers to work done at another's behest and on another's behalf. Indeed, it is most often translated "serve," and its two most common usages denote bound labor and human service of deities. Bound labor takes various forms, enslaved and remunerated, but is almost universally subordinated. Examples include indentured servitude, household and debt slavery, Israelite slavery in Egypt, corvée, and vassalage (*HALOT*, 2:774). Only a few usages refer to labor done freely and for oneself, including in the Sabbath commandments (Exodus 20:9, 34:21; Deuteronomy. 5:13), and several other occurrences of the stock phrase "work the ground" (Deuteronomy 21:4, 28:39; Zechariah 13:5; Proverbs 12:11, 28:19).

The verb *'ābad* also denotes the service of deities (Yahweh and other gods alike), though in such cases most translations render it "worship" (*HALOT*, 2:774). This translation implies a much more abstract and immaterial meaning, but there is evidence that service was differentiated from other types of worship and veneration. As described in Section 3.1, serving Yahweh involved the practical, physical work of preparing and maintaining shrines and administering the food service and other offerings and sacrifices. When Yahweh outlines the duties of the Aaronide priests in Numbers 18:7, he says: "You shall keep your priestly duties in everything regarding the altar and what is behind the curtain. Your service – the service of the gift – I give as your priesthood." The distinction is crucial in Joshua 22 when one group of Israelites confronts another about an altar they have built east of the Jordan River. They insist that they do not mean to provide offerings on it. It is only a *reminder* "to perform the service of Yahweh in his presence, [i.e., at Shiloh] with our burnt offerings and sacrifices and offerings of wellbeing" (Joshua 22:27; cf. Ezekiel 20:40). The types of worship they claim to perform there may be meaningful, but they do not qualify as service because they do not involve food service or sacrifice.

The verb *šāmar* is not as strictly hierarchical as *'ābad*, and it can refer to things done for oneself or someone else. It is noteworthy, however, that when it appears with *'ābad* it almost universally refers to service of deities and diligent performance of rites of the temple and sanctuary (Wells, 2023).[57] Thus, the dual mandate of the human to work and to keep the garden creates a resonance with other descriptions of offerings to Yahweh throughout the Bible.

Perhaps the most significant piece of evidence that humans were meant to tend a garden for the consumption of Yahweh and other divine beings is the very presence of the Tree of the Knowledge of Good and Bad. If the garden were planted for the sustenance of humans alone, planting and then forbidding an enticing tree would reflect callous caprice at best and moral entrapment at worst. This problem is intensified by readings that find in the Garden Story a narrative of the fall and original sin. In such readings, the sole purpose of the tree is to provide a moral hazard – introducing the possibility of damnation behind an attractive facade.

This thorny problem, however, is easily resolved if the food of the garden is first and foremost for divine consumption and only secondarily for humans. The garden is planted with trees whose fruit is appropriate for the consumption of gods, and the humans are permitted to eat from the subset of varietals that produce appropriate fruit for their needs and status. They are the help, and they are expected to eat like the help. In this reading, perhaps it is more surprising that only one of Yahweh's many trees is not meant for its human caretakers.

The prohibition and Yahweh's equivocation on the consequences are especially apt in light of the fruit's effects and Yahweh's interest in preserving a hierarchical labor relationship. The threat of death attached to the prohibition serves as the strongest possible deterrent intended to keep the humans in their place. It is not, as the reader discovers, for their own good, but to prevent them from gaining the knowledge it holds and taking one step closer to godhood.[58]

---

[57] See Deuteronomy. 11:16 12:30; 13:4; Joshua 22:5; 1 Kings 9:6; Jeremiah 16:11 for the former and Numbers 3:7, 3:8, 8:26, 18:7; Malachi 3:14 for the latter. Exceptions are 2 Samuel 22, where the two have different subjects, and Hosea 12:12, where they have different objects.

[58] Thus, my interpretation differs from ones like Kelly (2022), who has recently argued that Yahweh's prohibition was not a commandment in a legal sense but a warning based on natural consequences. That is, Yahweh knows that eating the fruit will preclude the humans from gaining eternal life and warns them not to eat of it for their own protection. Thus, it is a pragmatic injunction, not a moral one. This proposal solves the problem of moral entrapment but does not explain why Yahweh planted this tree in the garden in the first place. As an analogy, I have warned my children not to eat mushrooms they find growing wild for their own protection, but I have never planted poisonous mushrooms in my own garden and do not control where or when

When the humans do eat the fruit, however, Yahweh shows the threat to be overstated. Killing them does not suit Yahweh's interests, as it would put him out of a workforce. As part of his comparisons with administrative orders in neo-Babylonian temples, Wells (2020: 646–51) shows that such orders often included such conditional verdicts – articulations of the strongest possible penalty for an infraction that could be mitigated or abrogated at the supervisor's discretion.

The portrait that emerges, then, is one of Yahweh as master and supervisor – the owner of an estate who also takes part in its day-to-day affairs. It is not an especially sympathetic or flattering portrayal. Like *Atraḫasis*, the tale takes a critical, even satirical view of the god(s) while at the same time affirming the inevitability of a life spent in service to them. Unlike in *Atraḫasis*, whose deities have unique personalities and approaches to leadership, Yahweh makes all the decisions here, with a nameless, faceless divine community acting only as audience to his pronouncements. At times, it seems that Yahweh's character displays a certain incoherence or inconstancy, as the motivations and actions of multiple Mesopotamian deities had to be collapsed into a single agent. However, Yahweh is navigating a path that ensures continued food provision while also maintaining the subordinated position of the human labor force. He may not anticipate or plan for every eventuality but responds to events with a mixture of discipline and clemency that best keeps the humans productive and in line.

3.3 Summary of the Southern Levant

Archaeological and biblical evidence from the southern Levant present some incongruities not observed in Mesopotamia. In Mesopotamia, the system of temple households was deeply rooted and relatively consistent, notwithstanding local variations in practice. Thus, the creation mythology included the god's design for a society that reflected these long-standing institutions and the economic activities that supplied them. Biblical texts, on the other hand, betray a deep split on the topic of temples and offerings. Most biblical texts support the idea of a single, glorious abode on earth that hosts the approved service of Yahweh. The Yahwistic (J) source, however, along with the Elohist (E) and some portions of the southern Levantine populace, endorsed serving Yahweh with offerings at any altar constructed for the purpose.

Surprisingly, it is J that reflects the labor creation motif in its creation story, not P, D, or any of the other temple-centric sources. Those sources, with their

---

they grow. IF Yahweh planted this tree in a garden otherwise for the humans' express enjoyment, it was a choice that carries some moral responsibility.

great house and need to funnel surplus inward to support it, would have accommodated a mythological justification of extractive arrangements well. J's system supports fewer people and would require less surplus extraction overall. It acknowledges the necessity of extraction to serve Yahweh but resists the ideas of an entrenched class of religious professionals and of state control and exploitation. Thus, the Garden Story focuses on Yahweh as the beneficiary of extraction and on the labor relationship between Yahweh and his human worshippers. This, perhaps, is the religious expression of the kinship-based survival-subsistence economy, resisting extractive regimes or freed from them in a time of collapse. It is still the obligation of humankind to provide food to the deity, but not through (or to) earthly institutions.

4 Conclusions

Ritual is not separate from economics, and both are inextricably connected with mythmaking. As sets of materially instantiated practices that require labor and resources, rituals exist within, rely on, and influence broader economic practices in society. Throughout the ancient Middle East, rituals of divine service were particularly resource intensive. Housing, feeding, and otherwise tending to the gods required more labor and material resources than the ritual professionals produced, and the great institutions of temple and palace worked together to supply themselves from the surplus of the people. They employed many means to do so, from the violent and coercive to the transactional and voluntary.

Violence always backstopped the extractive system, but it ran more smoothly when there was willing cooperation. As such, the temple and palace both took great pains to manufacture consent using rhetoric and ideology. According to the ideology of divine service, it was the gods at whose command and for whose benefit extraction was undertaken. Kingship and priesthood were offices designed to orchestrate the production, collection, and provision of goods and labor to their divine masters. Thus, it was not only the right of temple and palace to engage in economic extraction but also their duty and their obligation. They were instrumental intermediaries, not exploitative elites.

The labor creation motif was not the only avenue by which this message was conveyed, but it certainly fit within the broad array of methods by which it was articulated and disseminated.

Atraḫasis and *Enki and Ninmaḫ* present the fullest case for the necessity of divine service, emerging as it did from bitter contestation among the gods and surviving Enlil's reckless attempt to destroy it. *Enūma Eliš* notes the creation of humankind for divine service almost as an afterthought, included and assumed without needing to be detailed or defended. The Garden of Eden story likewise assumes that humans were created to labor and provision their god but differs in its avoidance of the intermediary institutions of temple and palace. Giving up some portion of production was necessary, but only to support Yahweh, not an intermediary class of professionals.

From a distance of several millennia, it is impossible to know how important or effective creation myths were in upholding the ideology of divine service. The labor creation myths were first laid down in text in the second millennium and were copied, adapted, and rewritten thereafter, but this tells us little about how far the stories or their message about the created purpose of humankind propagated outside of elite literary circles. We do not know whether these narratives served primarily to reinforce the self-concept of the extractive classes or whether they were intended to spread and strengthen the ideology of divine service among productive agricultural and pastoral workers. How many farmers and shepherds in the fields of Mesopotamia and the southern Levant relinquished the fruits of their labor out of true belief in the ideology of divine service? How many due to the threat or reality of violence from overseers and soldiers? The perspectives of such people and their variety of motivations are lost to history, but in the production of creation mythology we find, among other things, concerted attempts to influence them from above.

References

Abusch, I. Tzvi. 1998. "Ghost and God: Some Observations on the Babylonian Understanding of Human Nature." In *Self, Soul, and Body in Religious Experience*. Edited by Albert I. Baumgarten, Jan Assmann, and Guy G. Stroumsa. Brill. 363–83.

———. 2007. "Biblical Accounts of Prehistory: Their Meaning and Formation." In *Bringing the Hidden to Light: The Process of Interpretation. Studies in Honor of Stephen A. Geller*. Edited by Kathryn Kravitz and Diane M. Sharon. Eisenbrauns. 1–17.

———. 2020. "Sacrifice in Mesopotamia." In *Essays in Babylonian and Biblical Literature and Religion*. Brill. 56–64.

Altman, Peter, ed. 2016. *Economics in Persian Period Biblical Texts: Their Interactions with Economic Developments in the Persian Period and Earlier Biblical Texts*. Mohr Siebeck.

Baden, Joel. 2012. *The Composition of the Pentateuch: Renewing the Documentary Hypothesis*. Yale University Press.

Bastani, Aaron. 2019. *Fully Automated Luxury Communism: A Manifesto*. Verso.

Batto, Bernard. 2013. "The Sleeping God: An Ancient Near Eastern Motif of Divine Sovereignty." In *In the Beginning: Essays on Creation Motifs in the Ancient Near East and the Bible*. Eisenbrauns. 140–57.

Beaulieu, Paul-Alain. 1990. "Cuts of Meat for Nebuchadnezzar." *Nabû* 93: 121.

Black, J. A., G. Cunningham, J. Ebeling, et al. 1998–2006. The Electronic Text Corpus of Sumerian Literature (ETCSL). Oxford. http://etcsl.orinst.ox.ac.uk/.

Boer, Roland. 2015. *The Sacred Economy of Ancient Israel*. Westminster John Knox Press.

———. 2023. "Production and Allocation in Ancient Southwest Asian Economics." In *Economics and Empire in the Ancient Near East*. Edited by Matthew J. M. Coomber. Wipf and Stock. 44–74.

Bottéro, Jean. 2001. *Religion in Ancient Mesopotamia*. Trans. Teresa Lavender Fagan. Chicago: University of Chicago Press.

Bourdieu, Pierre. 1984. *Distinction: A Social Critique of the Judgment of Taste*. Trans. Richard Nice. Harvard University Press.

Brisch, Nicole. 2017. "To Eat Like a God: Religion and Economy in Old Babylonian Nippur." In *At the Dawn of History: Ancient Near Eastern Studies in Honour of J. N. Postgate*. Edited by Yagmur Heffron, Adam Stone, and Martin Worthington. Eisenbrauns. 43–53.

Castellino, George R. 1994. "The Origins of Civilization according to Biblical and Cuneiform Texts." in *I Studied Inscriptions from Before the Flood: Ancient Near Eastern, Literary, and Linguistic Approaches to Genesis 1–11*. Edited by Richard S. Hess and David Toshio Tsumura. Eisenbrauns. 74–95.

Ceccarelli, Manuel. 2016. *Enki und Ninmaḫ: Eine Mythische Ehrzählung in Sumerische Sprache*. Mohr Siebeck.

Coomber, Matthew J. M., ed. 2023. *Economics and Empire in the Ancient Near East*. Guide to the Bible and Economics 1. Eugene, OR: Cascade Books.

Da Riva, Rosio. 2017. "The Figure of Nabopolassar in Late Achaemenid and Hellenistic Historiographic Tradition: BM 34793 and CUA 90." *JNES* 76, 1: 75–92.

Dalley, Stephanie. 2000. *Myths from Mesopotamia: Creation, the Flood, Gilgamesh, and Others*. Revised ed. Oxford University Press.

Dassow, Eva von. 2011. "Freedom in Ancient Near Eastern Societies." In *The Oxford Handbook of Cuneiform Culture*. Edited by Karen Radner and Eleanor Robson. Oxford University Press. 205–24.

———. 2014. "Awīlum and Muškenum in the Age of Hammurabi." In *La famille dans le Proche-Orient ancien: réalités, symbolismes, et images: Proceedings of the 55th Rencontre assyriologique internationale at Paris, 6–9 July 2009*. Edited by Lionel Marti. Eisenbrauns. 291–308.

DeGrado, Jessie. 2020. "An Infelicitous Feast: Ritualized Consumption and Divine Rejection in Amos 6.1–7." *JSOT* 45: 178–97.

Dossin, Georges. 1938. "Un rituel du culte d'Ištar provenant de Mari." *RA* 35, 1: 1–13.

Earle, Timothy K. 2002. *Bronze Age Economics: The Beginnings of Political Economies*. Westview Press.

Farber, Zev. 2019. "Israelite Festivals: From Cyclical Time Celebrations to Linear Time Commemorations." *Religions* 4: 19.

Faust, Avraham. 2010. "The Archaeology of the Israelite Cult: Questioning the Consensus." *BASOR* 360: 23–35.

———. 2019. "Israelite Temples: Where Was Israelite Cult Not Practiced, and Why." *Religions* 10 (106): 26.

Feldman, Liane. 2020a. *The Story of Sacrifice: Ritual and Narrative in the Priestly Source*. Mohr Siebeck.

———. 2020b. "The Idea and Study of Sacrifice in Ancient Israel." *Religion Compass* 14 (12): 1–14.

———. 2023. *The Consuming Fire: The Complete Priestly Source from Creation to the Promised Land*. University of California Press.

Foster, Benjamin R. 2005. *Before the Muses: An Anthology of Akkadian Literature*. 3rd ed. CDL Press.

Frymer-Kensky, Tikva. 2006a. "Atraḫasis: An Introduction." In *Studies in Bible and Feminist Criticism*. JPS Scholars of Distinction Series. Jewish Publication Society. 5–18.

———. 2006b. "The Atraḫasis Epic and Its Significance for Our Understanding of Genesis 1–9." In *Studies in Bible and Feminist Criticism*. JPS Scholar of Distinction Series. Jewish Publication Society. 51–66.

Gertz, Jan C., Bernard M. Levinson, Dalit Rom-Shiloni, and Konrad Schmid, eds. 2016. *The Formation of the Pentateuch: Bridging the Academic Cultures of Europe, Israel, and North America*. Mohr Siebeck.

Gilboa, Ayelet. 2013. "The Southern Levant (Cisjordan) during the Iron Age I Period." In *The Oxford Handbook of the Archaeology of the Levant, c. 8000 to 332 BCE*. Edited by Ann E. Killebrew and Margreet Steiner. Oxford University Press. 624–48.

Godelier, Maurice. 1986. *The Mental and the Material: Thought, Economy, and Society*. London: Verso.

Grant, Deena. 2015. "Fire and the Body of Yahweh." *JSOT* 40: 139–61.

Greenstein, Edward L. 2002. "God's Golem: The Creation of the Human in Genesis 2." In *Creation in Jewish and Christian Tradition*. JSOTSupp. 319. Edited by Henning Graf and Yair Hoffman. Sheffield Academic. 218–39.

Greer, Jonathan S. 2013. *Dinner at Dan: Biblical and Archaeological Evidence for Sacred Feasts at Iron Age II Tel Dan and Their Significance*. Leiden: Brill.

Greer, Jonathan S. 2019a. "The Zooarchaeology of Ancient Israelite Religion." *Religions* 10 (254): 19.

———. 2019b. "The Priestly Portion in the Hebrew Bible: Its Ancient Near Eastern Background and Its Implications for the Composition of P." *JBL* 138 (2): 263–84.

Halpern, Baruch. 1996. "Sybil, or the Two Nations? Archaism, Alienation, and the Elite Redefinition of Traditional Culture in Judah in the 8th–7th Centuries B.C.E." In *The Study of the Ancient Near East in the Twenty-First Century: The William Foxwell Albright Centennial Conference*. Edited by Jerrold S. Cooper and Glenn M. Schwartz. Eisenbrauns. 291–334.

Hamori, Esther J. 2008. *When Gods Were Men: The Embodied God in Biblical and Near Eastern Literature*. De Gruyter.

Haran, Menachem. 1978. *Temples and Temple Service in Ancient Israel: An Inquiry into the Character of Cult Phenomena and the Historical Setting of the Priestly School*. Clarendon.

Heffron, Yagmur. 2014. "Revisiting Noise (*rigmu*) in Atra-Hasis in Light of Baby Incantations." *JNES* 73 (1): 82–93.

Hemmer Gudme, and Anne Katrine de. 2020. "'If I Were Hungry, I Would Not Tell You' (Ps 50,12): Perspectives on the Care and Feeding of the Gods in the Hebrew Bible." *SJOT* 28: 172–84.

Hirth, Kenneth Gale. 2023. "Introducing Economy in the Ancient World." In *Economics and Empire in the Ancient Near East*. Edited by Matthew J. M. Coomber. Wipf and Stock. 12–43.

Hubert, Henri, and Marcel Mauss. 1964 (French original 1899). *Sacrifice: Its Nature and Functions*. Translated by W. D. Halls. University of Chicago Press.

Hudson, Michael. 2018. *… And Forgive Them Their Debts: Lending, Foreclosure, and Redemption from Bronze Age Finance to the Jubilee Year*. ISLET-Verlag.

Jacobsen, Thorkild. 1987. *The Harps that Once: Sumerian Poetry in Translation*. Yale University Press.

Kataja, Laura, and Robert Whiting. 1995. *Grants, Decrees and Gifts of the Neo-Assyrian Period*. State Archives of Assyria 12. Helsinki University Press.

Kelly, Joseph Ryan. 2022. "Does God Command and Punish in the Garden of Eden?" *VT* 72: 609–30.

Killebrew, Ann E. 2013. "Israel during the Iron Age II Period." In *The Oxford Handbook of the Archaeology of the Levant, c. 8000 to 332 BCE*. Edited by Ann E. Killebrew and Margreet Steiner. Oxford University Press. 730–42.

Kilmer, Anne Draffkorn. 1972. "The Mesopotamian Concept of Overpopulation and Its Solution as Represented in the Mythology." *Orientalia NS* 41: 160–77.

Kingsbury, Edwin C. 1963. "A Seven Day Ritual in the Old Babylonian Cult at Larsa." *Hebrew Union College Annual* 34: 1–34.

Kitts, Margo. 2022. *Sacrifice: Themes, Theories, and Controversies*. Elements in Religion and Violence. Cambridge University Press.

Klein, Jacob. 1997. "1.158. Enki and Ninmaḫ." In The *Context of Scripture, Vol. 1: Canonical Compositions from the Biblical World*. Edited by William Hallo and K. Lawson Younger. Brill. 516–18.

Koch, Ido. 2020. "Southern Levantine Temples during the Iron Age II: Towards a Multivocal Narrative." *Judaïsme Ancien/Ancient Judaism* 8: 325–44.

―――. 2023. "Sacred Architecture in Iron II Southern Levant." In *The Bloomsbury Handbook of Material Religion in the Ancient Near East and Egypt*. Edited by Nikola Laneri and Sharon R. Steadman. Bloomsbury Academic. 189–99.

Komoroczy, Géza. 1976. "Work and Strike of the Gods: New Light on the Divine Society in the Sumero-Akkadian Mythology." *Oikumene* 1: 11–37.

Koppen, Franz van. 2010. "The Scribe of the Flood Story and His Circle," In *The Oxford Handbook of Cuneiform Culture*. Edited by Karen Radner and Eleanor Robson. Oxford University press. 140–66.

Kozuh, Michael. 2014. *The Sacrificial Economy: Assessors, Contractors, and Thieves in the Management of Sacrificial Sheep at the Eanna Temple of Uruk (ca. 625–520 B.C.)*. Winona Lake, IN: Eisenbrauns.

Kvanvig, Helge S. 2014. *Primeval History: Babylonian, Biblical, and Enochic: An Intertextual Reading*. JSJSup 149. Brill.

Lambert, Wilfred G. 1969. "New Evidence for the First Line of Atra-ḫasīs." *OrNS* 38 (4): 533–8.

⸻. 1993. "Donations of Food and Drink to the Gods in Ancient Mesopotamia." In *Ritual and Sacrifice in the Ancient Near East*. Edited by J. Quaegebeur. Brill. 191–202.

⸻. 2008. "Mesopotamian Creation Stories." In *Imagining Creation*. Edited by Markham J. Geller and Mineke Schipper. Brill. 15–60.

⸻. 2013. *Babylonian Creation Myths*. Eisenbrauns.

Lambert, Wilfred G. and Alan R. Millard. 1969. *Atraḫasis: The Babylonian Story of the Flood*. Oxford University Press.

Langdon, Stephen. 1912. *Die Neubabylonischen Königsinschriften*. J. C. Hinrichs'sche Buchhandlung.

Leuchter, Mark. 2017. "The Levites in the Hebrew Bible." *Religion Compass* 11 (5–6): e12235.

Levine, Amy-Jill and Marc Zvi Brettler. 2020. *The Bible with and without Jesus: How Jews and Christians Read the Same Stories Differently*. Harper Collins.

Linssen, Mark J. H. 2004. *The Cults of Uruk and Babylon: The Temple Ritual Texts as Evidence for Hellenistic Cult Practice*. Brill.

Maggio, Michèle. 2012. "An Introduction to the Divine Statues of, and the Objects Belonging to, the Gods in Mesopotamia during the Old Babylonian Period (c. 2000–1595 BCE)." In *Materiality and Social Practice: Transformative Capacities of Intercultural Encounters*. Oxbow Books. 213–20.

Makkay, János. 1983. "The Origins of the Temple Economy as Seen in the Light of Prehistoric Evidence." *Iraq* 45: 1–6.

Mandell, Alice. 2022. "Genesis and Its Ancient Literary Analogues." In *The Cambridge Companion to Genesis*. Edited by Bill T. Arnold. Cambridge University Press. 121–47.

McClymond, Kathryn. 2008. *Beyond Sacred Violence: A Comparative Study of Sacrifice*. Johns Hopkins University Press.

McCutcheon, Russell. 2024. *Critics, Not Caretakers: Redescribing the Public Study of Religion*. 2nd ed. Routledge.

Menzel, Brigitte. 1981. *Assyrische Tempel*. 2 vols. Pontifical Biblical Institute.

Meyers, Carol L. 1988. *Discovering Eve: Ancient Israelite Women in Context*. Oxford University Press.

— 2012. *Rediscovering Eve: Ancient Israelite Women in Context*. Oxford University Press.

Michalowski, Piotr. 1990. "Presence at the Creation." In *Lingering over Words: Studies in Ancient Near Eastern Literature in Honor of William Moran*. Edited by Tzvi Abusch, John Huehnergard, and Piotr Steinkeller. Scholars Press. 381–96.

Mieroop, Marc van de. 1989. "Gifts and Tithes to the Temple in Ur." In *Dumu-e2-dub-ba-a: Studies in Honor of Åke W. Sjöberg*. Edited by Hermann Behrens, Darlene Loding, and Martha T. Roth. University of Penn Museum. 397–401.

Milgrom, Jacob. 1990. Numbers = Ba-Midbar: The Traditional Hebrew Text with the *New JPS Translation*. JPS Torah Commentary 4. Jewish Publication Society.

— 1991. *Leviticus: A New Translation with Introduction and Commentary*. Anchor Bible 3A. Doubleday.

Milli, Salvatore, and Luca Forti. 2019. "Geology and Palaeoenvironment of Nasiriyah Area/Southern Mesopotamia." In *Abu Tbeirah Excavations I. Area 1: Last Phase and Building A – Phase 1*. Edited by Licia Romano and Franco D'Agostino. Collana Materiali e documenti 44. Sapienza. 21–38.

Moran, William L. 1970. "The Creation of Man in Atrahasis I 192–248." *BASOR* 200: 48–56.

— 1971. "Atrahasis: The Babylonian Story of the Flood." *Biblica* 52: 51–61.

Morehart, Christopher T. and Kristin De Lucia, eds. 2015. *Surplus: The Politics of Production and the Strategies of Everyday Life*. University of Colorado Press.

Nam, Roger. 2012. *Portrayals of Economic Exchange in the Book of Kings*. Brill.

Oppenheim. A. Leo. 1956. "The Interpretation of Dreams in the Ancient Near East: With a Translation of an Assyrian Dream Book." *Transactions of the American Philosophical Society* 46: 179–373.

— 1977. *Ancient Mesopotamia: Portrait of a Dead Civilization*. Revised ed. University of Chicago Press.

Pettinato, Giovanni. 1968. "Die Bestrafung des Menschengeschlechts durch die Sinflut: die erste Tafel des Atramhasis-Epos eröffnet eine neue Einsicht in die Motivation dieser Strafe." *Orientalia NS* 37: 165–200.

Polanyi, Karl. 1944. *The Great Transformation: The Political and Economic Origins of Our Time*. Farrar and Rinehart.

———. 1957. *Trade and Market in the Early Empires: Economies in History and Theory*. Free Press.

Pollack, Susan. 1999. *Ancient Mesopotamia: The Eden that Never Was*. Cambridge University Press.

Pongratz-Leisten, Beate. 2012. "Sacrifice in the Ancient Near East: Offering and Sacred Killing." In *Sacred Killing: The Archaeology of Sacrifice*. Edited by Anne Porter and Glenn M. Schwartz. Eisenbrauns. 290–305.

Postgate, J. N. 1992. *Early Mesopotamia: Society and Economy at the Dawn of History*. London: Routledge.

Richards, E. G. 2012. "Calendars." In *Explanatory Supplement to the Astronomical Almanac*. 3rd ed. Edited by S. E. Urban and P. K. Seidelmann. University Science Books. 585–624.

Robbins, Ellen. 1996. "Tabular Sacrifice Records and the Cultic Calendar of Neo-Babylonian Uruk." *JCS* 48: 61–87.

Roth, Martha T. 2013. "On *Mār awilim* in the Old Babylonian Law Codes." *JNES* 72 (2): 267–72.

Rubio, Gonzalo. 2013. "Time before Time: Primeval Narratives in Early Mesopotamian Literature." In *Time and History in the Ancient Near East: Proceedings of the 56th Rencontre Assyriologique Internationale at Barcelona 26–30 July 2010*. Edited by Lluis Feliu, J. Llop, A. Millet Albà, and Joaquin Sanmartín. Eisenbrauns. 3–17.

Sachs, Abraham. 1969. "Daily Sacrifices to the Gods of the City of Uruk." In *Ancient Near Eastern Texts Relating to the Old Testament*. 3rd ed. Edited by James B. Pritchard. Princeton University Press. 343–5.

Sallaberger, Walter. 2007. "The Palace and the Temple in Babylonia." in *The Babylonian World*. Edited by Gwendolyn Leick. Routledge. 265–75.

Salt-N-Pepa. 1991. "Let's Talk About Sex." *Blacks' Magic*. Next Plateau.

Sasson, Aharon. 2010. *Animal Husbandry in Ancient Israel: A Zooarchaeological Perspective on Livestock Exploitation, Herd Management, and Economic Strategies*. Equinox.

Schloen, J. David. 2001. *The House of the Father as Fact and Symbol: Patrimonialism in Ugarit and the Ancient Near East*. Brill.

Schmitt, Rüdiger. 2014. "A Typology of Iron Age Cult Places." In *Family and Household Religion: Toward a Synthesis of Old Testament Studies, Archaeology, Epigraphy, and Cultural Studies*. Edited by Rainer Albertz, Beth Alpert Nakhai, Saul M. Olyan, and Rüdiger Schmitt. Eisenbrauns. 265–86.

Scott, Marissa. 2021. "A Zooarchaeological Study of Animal Sacrifice in the Bronze and Iron Age Southern Levant." MA Thesis. Pennsylvania State University.

Scurlock, JoAnn. 2002. "Animal Sacrifice in Ancient Mesopotamian Religion." In *A History of the Animal World in the Ancient Near East*. Edited by Billie Jean Collins. Brill. 389–403.

⎯⎯⎯. 2006a. "The Techniques of the Sacrifice of Animals in Ancient Israel and Ancient Mesopotamia: New Insights through Comparison, Part 1." *Andrews University Seminary Studies* 44 (1): 13–49.

⎯⎯⎯. 2006b. "The Techniques of the Sacrifice of Animals in Ancient Israel and Ancient Mesopotamia: New Insights through Comparison, Part 2." *Andrews University Seminary Studies* 44 (2): 241–64.

Seabright, Paul. 2024. *The Divine Economy: How Religions Compete for Wealth, Power, and People*. Princeton University Press.

Selz, Gebhard J. 2007. "Power, Economy, and Social Organization in Babylonia." In *The Babylonian World*. Edited by Gwendolyn Leick. Routledge. 276–88.

Seri, Andrea. 2006. "The Fifty Names of Marduk in Enūma Eliš." *JAOS* 126: 507–19.

⎯⎯⎯. 2014. "Borrowings to Create Anew: Intertextuality in the Babylonian Poem of Creation, Enūma Eliš." *JAOS* 134: 89–106.

Sharlach, Tonia. 2004. *Provincial Taxation in the Ur III State*. Brill.

Sigrist, Marcel. 1984. Les Satukku Dans l'Ešumeša Durant La Période d'Isin et Larsa. Malibu: Undena.

Smith, Mark S. 2014. *How Human Is God? Seven Questions about God and Humanity in the Bible*. Liturgical Press.

⎯⎯⎯. 2015. "The Three Bodies of God in the Hebrew Bible." *JBL* 134: 471–88.

Sommer, Benjamin. 2009. *The Bodies of God in Ancient Israel*. Cambridge University Press.

Stackert, Jeffrey. 2012. "Sacrifice, Ancient Near East." *Encyclopedia of Ancient History*. https://onlinelibrary.wiley.com/doi/full/10.1002/9781444338386.wbeah01167

Staples, Jason A. 2021. *The Idea of Israel in Second Temple Judaism: A New Theory of People, Exile, and Jewish Identity*. Cambridge University Press.

Stavrokopoulou, Francesca. 2021. *God: An Anatomy*. Penguin/Random House.

Steinkeller, Piotr. 2013. "Corvée Labor in Ur-III Times." In *From the 21st Century BC to the 21st Century AD: Proceedings of the International Conference on Neo-Sumerian Studies Held in Madrid 22–24 July 2010*. Edited by Steven Garfinkel and Manuel Molina. Eisenbrauns. 347–424.

Stone, Elizabeth C. 2013. "The Organization of a Sumerian Town: The Physical Remains of Ancient Social Systems." In *The Sumerian World*. Edited by Harriet Crawford. Routledge. 156–78.

Streck, Michael P. and Nathan Wasserman. 2005–2025. Sources of Early Akkadian Literature (SEAL). http://seal.huji.ac.il.

Thureau-Dangin, F. 1921. *Rituels Accadiens*. Louvre.

Tsumura, David Toshio. 1994. "Genesis and Ancient Near Eastern Stories of Creation and Flood: An Introduction." In *I Studied Inscriptions from Before the Flood: Ancient Near Eastern, Literary, and Linguistic Approaches to Genesis 1–11*. Edited by Richard S. Hess and David Toshio Tsumura. Eisenbrauns. 27–57.

Uehlinger, Christoph. 2015. "Distinctive or Diverse? Conceptualizing Ancient Israelite Religion in Its Southern Levantine Setting." *HeB/AI* 4 (1): 1–24.

Waerzeggers, Caroline. 2010. *The Ezida Temple at Borsippa: Priesthood, Cult, Archives*. Nederlands Instituut voor het Nabije Oosten.

Wellhausen, Julius. 1878. *Geschichte Israels*. G. Reimer.

Wells, Bruce. 2020. "Death in the Garden of Eden." *JBL* 139 (4). 639–60.

2023. "The Oblates of Eden: Babylonian Temples and the Untold Backstory of Adam and Eve." Lecture delivered in Frankfurt, Germany.

Wenham, Gordon. 1987. *Genesis*. Word Biblical Commentary 1. Word Books.

Westenholz, Aage. 2010. "Enki and Ninmah." In *A Woman of Valor: Jerusalem Ancient Near Eastern Studies in Honor of Joan Goodnick Westenholz*. Edited by Wayne Horowitz, Uri Gabbay, and Filip Vukosavović. Biblioteca del Próximo Oriente Antiguo 8.: Consejo Superior de Investigaciones Científicas. 202–05.

Westenholz, Joan Goodnick. 2013. "In the Service of the Gods: The Ministering Clergy." In *The Sumerian World*. Edited by Harriet Crawford. Routledge. 246–74.

Wright, David P. 2015. "Profane versus Sacrificial Slaughter: The Priestly Recasting of the Yahwist Flood Story." In *Current Issues in Priestly and Related Literature: The Legacy of Jacob Milgrom and Beyond*. Edited by Roy E. Gane and Ada Taggar-Cohen. SBL Press. 125–54.

Yee, Gale A. 1999. "Gender, Class, and the Social-Scientific Study of Genesis 2–3." *Semeia* (87): 177–92.

2017. "'He Will Take the Best of your Fields': Royal Feasts and Rural Extraction." *JBL* 136 (4): 821–38.

Zevit, Ziony. 2001. *The Religions of Ancient Israel: A Synthesis of Parallactic Approaches*. Continuum.

2013. *What Really Happened in the Garden of Eden?* Yale University Press.

Acknowledgments

This Element is intended to be useful for both specialists and nonspecialists in the languages of the ancient Middle East, so words and phrases in the original languages are transliterated into Latin characters. When individual words are given to show patterns in word usage, they are lemmatized so that affixes and derived forms do not obscure basic lexical correspondences. Mimation is included only when Akkadian text is quoted, not in lemmatized forms. Transliteration conventions and abbreviations follow *The SBL Handbook of Style, 2nd Edition*. All translations are the author's unless otherwise noted. Abbreviations follow the *SBL Handbook of Style, 2d ed.* And the CDLI Wiki "Abbreviations for Assyriology."

I am grateful to many interlocutors for reading and responding to earlier drafts of this Element, in whole or in part. To Daniel, the Lyft driver whose question about Anunnaki prompted a conversation on divine unionization and labor politics; to Anthony Soo Hoo for his detailed and generous response to an early draft paper; to the Colloquium for Biblical and Near Eastern Studies for incisive and generative discussion of its arguments; to Jessie DeGrado for help finding images, producing maps, and for writing company; to Liane Feldman for answering questions about sacrifice; to Ido Koch for assistance with images and southern Levantine archaeology; to Jonathan Greer for providing archaeological images; and to the series editors for entertaining this unusual project and for orienting me to relevant literature in economic anthropology. Thanks also to William Brown for feedback throughout the writing process. This Element, perhaps more than anything else I have yet written, reflects the influence of Tzvi Abusch on my perspective and scholarship, and I thank him for his years of mentorship and support. All remaining errors, flaws, and shortcomings are my own.

Cambridge Elements

Ancient and Pre-modern Economies

Kenneth G. Hirth
The Pennsylvania State University

Ken Hirth's research focuses on the development of ranked and state-level societies in the New World. He is interested in political economy and how forms of resource control lead to the development of structural inequalities. Topics of special interest include: exchange systems, craft production, settlement patterns, and preindustrial urbanism. Methodological interests include: lithic technology and use-wear, ceramics, and spatial analysis.

Timothy Earle
Northwestern University

Timothy Earle is an economic anthropologist specializing in the archaeological studies of social inequality, leadership, and political economy in early chiefdoms and states. He has conducted field projects in Polynesia, Peru, Argentina, Denmark, and Hungary. Having studied the emergence of social complexity in three world regions, his work is comparative, searching for the causes of alternative pathways to centralized power.

Emily J. Kate
University of Vienna

Emily Kate is bioarchaeologist with training in radiocarbon dating, isotopic studies, human osteology, and paleodemography. Having worked with projects from Latin America and Europe, her interests include the manner in which paleodietary trends can be used to assess shifts in social and political structure, the affect of migration on societies, and the refinement of regional chronologies through radiocarbon programs.

About the Series

Elements in Ancient and Pre-modern Economies is committed to critical scholarship on the comparative economies of traditional societies. Volumes either focus on case studies of well documented societies, providing information on domestic and institutional economies, or provide comparative analyses of topical issues related to economic function. Each Element adopts an innovative and interdisciplinary view of culture and economy, offering authoritative discussions of how societies survived and thrived throughout human history.

Cambridge Elements

Ancient and Pre-modern Economies

Elements in the Series

Ancient and Pre-modern Economies of the North American Pacific Northwest
Anna Marie Prentiss

The Aztec Economy
Frances F. Berdan

Shell Money: A Comparative Study
Mikael Fauvelle

A Historical Ethnography of the Enga Economy of Papua New Guinea
Polly Wiessner, Akii Tumu and Nitze Pupu

Ancient Maya Economies
Scott R. Hutson

Nordic Bronze Age Economies
Christian Horn, Knut Ivar Austvoll, Magnus Artursson and Johan Ling

Economies of the Inca World
R. Alan Covey and Jordan Dalton

The Shang Economy
Roderick Campbell

Reading Creation Myths Economically in Ancient Mesopotamia and Israel
Eric J. Harvey

A full series listing is available at: www.cambridge.org/EAPE

Printed by Integrated Books International,
United States of America